CW01662418

PENG

SKIL

Ronnie Screwvala is a first-generation entrepreneur who failed his Bachelor of Commerce course in college, but that did not deter him from setting out in the world of business on his own at a time when there was no ecosystem for entrepreneurs. He pioneered cable TV, went on to build one of the largest toothbrush operations in India and thereafter, the very successful media and entertainment company UTV. *Newsweek* termed him the 'Jack Warner of India', *Esquire* ranked him among the seventy-five most influential people of the twenty-first century and *Fortune* hailed him as 'Asia's 25 most powerful'. He is the co-founder of upGrad, which is India's largest online higher education company. Ronnie and his wife, Zarina, are founder–trustees of the Swades Foundation, a non-profit organization committed to improving the standard of living in rural areas. This is Ronnie's second book. His first, *Dream with Your Eyes Open*, was published in 2015. He lives in Mumbai with his wife, daughter, Trishya, and son-in-law, Suhail.

A NATIONAL BESTSELLER

SKILL IT, *KILL IT*

FAST-FORWARD YOUR CAREER WITH

RONNIE SCREWVALA

PENGUIN BUSINESS

An imprint of Penguin Random House

PENGUIN BUSINESS

USA | Canada | UK | Ireland | Australia
New Zealand | India | South Africa | China | Singapore

Penguin Business is part of the Penguin Random House group of companies whose addresses can be found at global.penguinrandomhouse.com

Published by Penguin Random House India Pvt. Ltd
4th Floor, Capital Tower 1, MG Road,
Gurugram 122 002, Haryana, India

Penguin Random House India

First published in Portfolio by Penguin Random House India 2021
Published in Penguin Business 2022

Copyright © Ronnie Screwvala 2021

All rights reserved

10 9 8 7

The views and opinions expressed in this book are the author's own and the facts are as reported by him which have been verified to the extent possible, and the publishers are not in any way liable for the same.

ISBN 9780143454564

For sale in the Indian Subcontinent only

Typeset in Sabon by Manipal Technologies Limited, Manipal
Printed at Replika Press Pvt. Ltd, India

This book is sold subject to the condition that it shall not, by way of trade or otherwise, be lent, resold, hired out, or otherwise circulated without the publisher's prior consent in any form of binding or cover other than that in which it is published and without a similar condition including this condition being imposed on the subsequent purchaser.

www.penguin.co.in

FSC
www.fsc.org
MIX
Paper from responsible sources
FSC® C016779

Contents

Acknowledgements vii
Introduction ix

1. Communication Is Everything, Everything Is Communication 1
2. Strive to Be a Storyteller 17
3. You Don't Have to Be Big to Think Big 29
4. All Shine, No Whine 42
5. The New LOL: Listen, Observe, Learn 53
6. Empathy Is a Sign of Strength, Not Weakness 66
7. Future-Proof Your Career 76
8. The Multitasking Myth 89
9. 'Stability' Is a Slippery Slope 101
10. From Clashes to Connections 112
11. Batteries and Vampires 124
12. The One Thing You *Do* Control 139
13. Seek Guidance, Not Crutches 150

Afterword 161

Acknowledgements

Thank you, Wynton, for being such a great partner in co-writing this book. When we shortlisted the chapters and I said I wanted to narrate them in my own voice, I thought this was going to be a tough one but you made it all too easy.

Thanks, Namrata, for being a great support—your hard work, focus groups and interactions with those for whom this book is written gave us the right nuggets and triggered the exact points that are addressed in this book.

No amount of thanks is enough for my senior colleagues, mentioned below, who gave their time to share their expert advice and words of wisdom for every chapter.

To Amitabh Kant, CEO of NITI Aayog—our national think tank—and the voice of the institution that is catalysing economic development. Harsh Goenka, chairman of the $4 billion RPG Group. Kiran Mazumdar-Shaw, billionaire entrepreneur and chairperson of Biocon Limited. Ritesh Agarwal, founder, OYO, and the second-youngest billionaire in the world in 2020. Sanjeev Mehta, CMD of Hindustan Unilever Ltd, for his breadth of knowledge as one of the largest employers in India. Suneeta Reddy, MD, Apollo Group. Vani Kola, MD, Kalaari Capital, one of India's leading early-stage venture capital firms. And Vijay Shekar Sharma, founder, Paytm, ranked by *Time* magazine as one of the most influential people in the world.

Thank you to the ever-growing alumni at upGrad who bring out the raw ambition and need to excel in life and in their careers, and whose wise feedback and questioning led me to write the chapters in this book; thanks also to our fabulous 2500-strong team at upGrad that give their best to everything they do as they see the impact we make on the careers and lives of so many working professionals.

Thank you to my wife, Zarina, for always pointing me to the right North Star, of giving back the wisdom gained from my learnings and failures that triggered me to write this book and share my lessons. And thanks to my daughter, Trishya, who so well represents what young people around the world are thinking and doing today, with their hearts and minds in the right place. This inspires me to stay curious and reach out and connect with all of you.

Introduction

I refuse to waste your time. It's too valuable.

So let's get the bad news out of the way at the start.

Ready?

The days when a working professional could kick back, grow lazy, enter a comfort zone and be content with just 'stable' growth in her or his career are over.

As you probably know by now, getting a degree wasn't the finish line, it was just the beginning. Continuous learning is now the norm. I like to call it #LifeLongLearning. And upskilling alone won't give you a clear advantage in the job market. Skilling is an overused buzzword! For most of us it seems to imply learning a new vocation or trying to get better at a skill, or getting trained in a particular skill you never had. Well, it's no longer enough. It will simply keep you relevant in your present job.

Now, the good news—*great* news, actually.

There *is* a set of skills that *will* give you a sizeable professional edge. Better still, these skills don't change over time, unlike endless software updates. Once you learn and perfect these abilities, they can catapult your career over the rest of the crowd. This won't happen overnight, of course. It will require self-motivation and personal determination. But obtaining these talents will rocket your ability to get the job you want, climb higher and faster in an organization, and maximize the meaningful impact you make for your family and community.

What are these 'magical' talents?

I'm talking about 'soft skills'—traits and abilities high-achieving professionals hone alongside their core fields of knowledge and expertise. Most people lack them, which is why companies find them so valuable and attractive. Know someone who can code with ease, but who struggles to communicate clearly? Or a data engineer with a knack for Python, Java, SQL or C++, but who lacks the confidence and ability to inspire or lead others? These people possess plenty of 'hard' knowledge, but they're missing the critical 'soft' skills that make all the difference in getting ahead.

It's not their fault. In fact, most of us are this way. I know I was. Growing up on Grant Road in Mumbai, I had studied basic subjects like math and science. But training for things like interviewing, negotiation, persuasion, consensus-building, emotional intelligence, oral and non-verbal communication . . . such lessons were non-existent. I realized if I wanted those abilities, I would have to learn them on my own. So, I did.

Then, after spending decades launching, running and scaling businesses, I understood that these soft skills are the key difference between the person who just gets a degree versus the person who gets the job (or promotion).

This isn't a theory. We know soft skills are game-changers for all aspiring professionals, and I've seen this throughout my career—as a founder, an employer and as a mentor. As I write this, upGrad has trained over a million learners across diverse fields and produced tens of thousands of graduates. We partner with innovative companies to place our high-skilled alumni. Then, through in-depth follow-up research, we track the arc of an individual's rise. Here's what our research has found—employees who report the highest career satisfaction and advancement are those with higher proficiencies in soft skills.

What you're about to read is not a self-help book. Plenty of those already exist. And besides, most of them say the same thing, just in slightly different ways. The goal of this book is to pull back the curtain on the professional world to give you an insider's view of the 'invisible' skills sought and rewarded by global businesses, top recruiters and leading CEOs. The way I've chosen to do this is by sharing stories, failures and personal learnings from my career and what I've observed around me. Through these chapters, I will address the massive changes we all need to prepare for and make across multiple sectors as we head into the 2020s and 2030s.

Before writing the book, I did interviews and focus groups with close to 1000 working professionals across the country, and the big questions and concerns that popped up were related to:

(a) the need for career guidance;
(b) help with soft skills;
(c) managing priorities and time better;
(d) the need for inspiration.

I have tried to deal with all this and more in the book.

We are on the verge of a dramatic shift in the workforce that will lead to changes in career paths not experienced before. Every job, every role will demand change. Change will need new learnings. Sales jobs will no longer be about making presentations or pitching but understanding data, lead generation and conversions. Marketing will not be about mature messaging but first knowing where to find your elusive customer and then communicating with the maximum clutter around them. Banking has changed 180 degrees in jobs the sector needs, and fintech and insurance tech is forcing us to move with the times. Even IT has in the last few years moved from processing to value additions. You get my point!

It's the decade and age of the specialist, the relocators, the solopreneurs, interpreneurs and entrepreneurs. Even the generalist will need to upgrade and learn. If you're not in the top 50 per cent of your company's team, your career is more likely to go sideways. Getting on to the lifelong learning train is no longer an option. Rounding off your professional expertise with stronger soft skills is where you can shine above the crowd.

Developing and sharpening your soft skills will put you on the fast track and enable you to stand out from the crowd, gain confidence and get ahead. The skills will give you additional power over and above your degree and area of knowledge (which everyone already has access to). Think of it this way—we all know that friend or colleague who was a bookworm in school and aced every exam in college, but remained socially awkward and insecure. They had all the right knowledge and degrees, but somehow struggled to succeed when they entered the real world. And then there's that other friend whose grades were average, who struggled in some classes, asked questions others thought were dumb, but was super confident and great with people. They somehow went on to achieve far more than anyone ever thought they would. What explains these two people's experiences?

Two words: soft skills. In this book, I'm going to introduce you to real people who taught themselves these vital abilities. If they can do it, so can you.

This book is not meant to be read just once, but several times throughout your career. Learning and polishing soft skills is a process that involves lifelong learning. There's no get-rich-quick method, and jugaad does not mean shortcuts. The way to get the most out of this book is to keep it handy, make notes whether you are reading it or listening to it, and feel free to go back and review points that struck a chord with you. Different chapters will mean different things to you at different points in your career. Put simply, this book's meaning will evolve as you do. I would really like this book to connect with the daughter and father, the son and mother, the patriarch and the working mom. I've written this with learnings that will resonate with everyone and make for great family dinner table conversation too.

So relax. Have fun. Scribble notes as you read. And together, let's up your game by making one of the biggest investments in yourself—the ability to raise the bar and to convey to others the knowledge, creativity, dreams and determination burning inside you.

Let's get to work!

1

Communication Is Everything, Everything Is Communication

Strong communicators are not born, they are made over time through practice and rehearsal. I should know. Of course, some people may be naturally gifted, but I was definitely not one of them.

I grew up in a lower middle-class family, and English was not my first language. I was lucky enough to go to an English-medium school, but English wasn't spoken most of the time in our household; Gujarati was. In fact, my parents actually sent me to voice and pronunciation classes to help me overcome my early struggles in learning the language. It was not cheap, but they were smart enough to know that paying for this soft skill would be even more valuable than spending on school fees. To say I was an awkward public speaker is putting it kindly.

In my teens, the importance of communication began to dawn on me. The cool, confident kids could tell funny stories and jokes. And the leaders of the class could give inspiring speeches, make friends easily and persuade people to see their point of view in debates. So I decided to do something about my weak communication skills. I signed up for debates, elocution classes and, later, theatre. Initially, I was a mess at all three. But then I learnt the most important communication lesson of all: rehearse, prepare and then hear yourself. Let me explain what I mean.

During a debate practice someone said, 'Wait a minute . . . wait a minute. Let me record you and let you hear yourself.' The first time I heard myself, I thought, 'My God, is this really how I sound?! It's awful!' But then I would rehearse, prepare some more, and then record and review my performance. Slowly but surely, I smoothed out the rough spots in my communication until it was clear, clean and crisp. It wasn't easy, but the more I heard my recorded voice, the more I knew I had to correct it, even if that meant standing in front of the mirror for hours, frustrated, till I eventually saw slow improvement. After that, it was all about practice and not forgetting how bad I was.

In college, I took the same approach to theatre and acting. Rehearsals were from 6 p.m. to 9 p.m. after a full day's work. I'd walk in tired and exhausted, but it was so much fun that by the time I left I was re-energized. Over and over and over again, we'd run through the same scenes in a play until it was perfect. And then the director would say, 'Okay, lovely. Let's take it again,' which meant starting from the beginning and doing it all over again. That experience taught me a lesson I've never forgotten—when it comes to communication, there's no such thing as being over-prepared.

Communication Is the #1 Skill for a Reason

If you think about it, communication is everything.

There are, of course, the obvious activities like speaking, texting and writing an email. But even when you're sitting silently, you're still communicating. In fact, sometimes when you're quiet, you're saying much *more* than when words are spilling out of your mouth. If you've ever been angry at someone and given them the 'silent treatment', you know exactly what I mean.

The simple fact is this: for humans, communication is unavoidable. It touches every dimension of the professional career world. Job interviews, resume writing, work presentations, emails, speeches, sales pitches, customer service, socializing with colleagues, team building—communication really is everything, because everything is a form of communication. I ask Vani Kola of Kalaari Capital for her views on the matter. She says, 'To me, communication is to convey, convince and carry others with you.' She's right, and that is why virtually every employer considers communication skills among the most desired employee attributes. As NITI Aayog CEO Amitabh Kant puts it: 'To successfully navigate one's career, we require an individual to engage with people, to communicate ideas, to build relationships.' But how?

Chances are, you're probably not a world-class public speaker or writer. If that's the case, breathe easy. You're in good company. In fact, 99.9 per cent of the 7.8 billion people on earth are not motivational speakers or award-winning writers.

Strong communicators are not born, they're self-made. I like what Sanjeev Mehta, CMD of Hindustan

Unilever (HUL), had to say on the topic. 'Not everyone is born with the gift of the gab, but effort can make you an excellent communicator.' What an encouraging insight.

With focused effort, you can dramatically and permanently boost your communication skills in ways that will forever raise the trajectory of your career. All that's required is a desire to improve and a willingness to put in the hours to make it happen. No one else can put in the preparation and practice time for you. But choosing not to improve one's communication skills isn't really an option in today's job market. 'If you expect people to build a career without effective communication skills, it's akin to attempting to travel internationally without a passport, it's not feasible,' Amitabh Kant added during our conversation. 'Therefore, communication skills are really key.'

If you want to be among the top 20 per cent of employees in your company, you will need to invest the time in practising and rehearsing your communication skills. Trust me, it's worth it, and will pay you back many times over.

Vani Kola says when she was in her thirties, as a young founder CEO, she went to a communication coach who trained TV anchors and did an intense learning programme. Vani says the coach stopped her every minute to tell her everything she did wrong. He taped her and made her watch herself. She says that was the best lesson on how to improve. To date, whenever she has a TED talk or speech, she tapes herself and watches it again and again. So, like I said, prepare, rehearse and listen to how you sound. When you do, you will take huge steps towards becoming a better communicator.

Structure, Knowing Your Audience and Avoiding Over-Speaking

We have all come across that guy at work who starts speaking, and then everyone silently groans: 'Oh no . . . here he goes again . . . now he will take ages to make a single point and go all over the place and ramble on and on.' Now ask yourself honestly, is that how people feel when you speak? The truth is that we can all be so much sharper and to the point in the way we talk to colleagues and during office meetings.

It all starts with organizing your thoughts. Strong communication is first and foremost about clarity. Before a sales and marketing meeting, for example, write down the three 'headline' points you want to cover. I asked Paytm founder Vijay Shekhar Sharma for his tips on the subject so I could share them with you. 'When you go on stage, give a talk, or address your team, you should not take more than three messages to give and never go with less than one message to give.' By focusing on a few core points, he says, you are better able to maintain your listeners' attention and drive home your points.

Then, practise and rehearse your three main messages. Say them out loud the night before and record yourself. Are you clear? Boring? If so, is there a way to make your sentences sparkle? Remember: practise, rehearse, listen to yourself speak. That's the way to sharpen your communication skills. And this is not just for a talk or lecture but for a meet or presentation too.

Next, consider your audience. When you're speaking to just one or two people, your tone can be casual and personal. But when you're in a group addressing or sharing information with your sales, marketing or HR team, or speaking up at a company town hall or webinar, you have to be more aware of your tone and language to connect with a diverse group. When I asked Tech Mahindra's CEO C.P. Gurnani about this, he offered a powerful insight. 'Let me be blasphemous and say communication is not important—CONNECTING is. For me, the first lesson in communication is empathy. Language is just a medium. Incidental. The gift is the ability to make someone your own by establishing mutual trust, respect and a connection.' One of the ways we can create the sort of connection C.P. mentions is to adjust and customize our message for different groups and audiences.

For example, if you have a blunt one-on-one style, you need to adjust it slightly to make sure that people who don't know you or your personality well aren't put off or think you're being rude. It's a small adjustment, but an important one.

Likewise, when you're speaking to a large group where people use and know multiple languages, speak the language you're most comfortable with. Trust me on this. The key is the way you do it. I have been in enough rooms where the conversation has been largely in Hindi, and I have chipped in in English. Earlier, people would laugh, 'Oh, there goes Ronnie . . . with his south Mumbai English!' But I would self-deprecatingly admit, 'My Hindi sucks so you'll please excuse this Parsi boy's language . . .' Everyone saw I wasn't embarrassed and I was just being natural, and forgot about it.

Another approach to overcoming linguistic challenges is to learn the language of one's peers. I loved the story

Amitabh Kant shared with me when he got selected for the Indian Administrative Service (IAS); he was in the Kerala cadre and worked in the state for over twenty-five years. He knew Hindi and English, but in Kerala, everyone spoke mostly in Malayalam. So he started learning the language from the first day he got there.

Soon, he found his ability to communicate was much better, and he was more effective than even local Malayali IAS officers. People loved it—and him. So remember: language isn't a barrier to communication, not making sense is. With the right amount of effort, you don't need to learn a new language, but you can use language to your advantage.

Finally, avoid 'over-speaking'. Make your point clearly and creatively. Then be quiet. If you go on and on, after a minute or two everyone at the table starts to think you're speaking just for the sake of 'impressing' people, and they stop listening. That is not good. As Kiran Mazumdar-Shaw, the founder–chairman of Biocon, told me, 'I always tell young people: keep to the point, don't stray, and don't give a very long-winded answer.' That's great advice. It's much better to keep your remarks short and crisp so that you leave your listeners wanting more.

Say Something Without Saying Anything

You've got a tightly structured presentation, have crafted your message to your audience, and know when to stop talking. Now it's time to look at one of the most overlooked aspects of communication: non-verbal communication. Facial expressions, hand gestures, body language, posture, eye contact—so many of the most powerful and impactful aspects of human communication occur without uttering a single word. This is particularly true in the workplace. Just listen to the things colleagues whisper to one another in the office lounge, breakroom or over lunch.

'He just *stares* at you blankly when you speak to him. He doesn't even *nod* to let you know he's listening. It's like talking to a wall!'

'She never *smiles*! Ever. What's up with that?'

'Did you see the way he *looked* at her? Totally inappropriate and unprofessional.'

'Have you noticed how she *makes faces* during team meetings? It's so rude and obnoxious.'

'He always sits with his *arms crossed*. Is he angry? Or just insecure?'

Throughout your career, you will come across dozens of comments like these. Yet, if you look at the emphasized words, you will see that none of them have anything to do with spoken or written communication; they're all based on silent signals. While many people find it easy to spot non-verbal behaviours and annoyances in others, most of us have a blind spot when it comes to recognizing them in ourselves.

> *'In my first job, I was always enthusiastic about speaking up in work meetings but would unknowingly roll my eyes when others spoke. I did not realize how rude I was being until my boss pointed it out.'*
>
> —Rohan (28), research analyst, Kanpur

Rohan was lucky to have a boss who gave him honest feedback, but what can *you* do to improve your own non-verbal communication? The first step to upping one's non-verbal game is to conduct a personal non-verbal audit. Who amongst your friends and family gives you the most honest feedback? Latch on to them. Ask them to observe you and keep giving you feedback. What irritates them about your non-verbal habits? How and when do you act or react in a way that paints you in poor light? Assure them you won't get upset or defensive at hearing the answer. Then, listen, absorb and assess. Gaining self-awareness of one's own non-verbal peculiarities is the first and most important step to reduce and eventually eliminate them.

Another critical aspect of strong non-verbal communication is eye contact. Let's be clear: if you're not making eye contact, you're not communicating. Eye contact makes the other person realize how genuine you are—that you're sincerely interested in connecting with them and their ideas. I asked Harsh Goenka, chairman, RPG Group, for his thoughts on the subject. 'One thing people don't do that I'd advise them to do is to have their body language right, and also eye contact; it's extremely important to maintain eye contact,' he explained. 'What's not that important is polished English. One of the best communicators I've met is cricketer Kapil Dev, who speaks very rustic English, but he is more convincing and has better power of communication than even a Shashi Tharoor.'

The other great thing about strong eye contact is that it makes up for so many other communication weaknesses one may have. You may be nervous, have a stutter or the worst pronunciation, but if you have strong and sincere eye contact, it will make up for the other deficiencies. Sometimes, due to culturally driven habits or the way you were raised, eye contact may not come naturally to you. But that's why the practise–rehearse–record yourself mantra is so important. Do that, and before you know it you'll pick up the skill in no time. Remember, eye contact does not mean staring blankly or aggressively at someone. You make a connection when you tell the person—I am totally focused on my conversation with you, and also, we are 'equals' in this. Looking down at the ground while speaking only shows you are not as confident as the person you're speaking to, and you know that's not true. Therefore, eye contact!

Non-verbal scholars also tell us that effective hand gestures and body language project confidence. For example, people who put their hands near or over their mouths when speaking are perceived as less confident. The word 'perceived' refers to how other people view or interpret something, regardless of whether their perspective is accurate or inaccurate. That's why non-verbal communication is so critical; you might not intend to send a negative message, but that doesn't mean people won't perceive something you do negatively. For example, not everyone who puts their hand near their face is self-conscious (who knows . . . they could just be scratching an itch!). But again, those gestures can send a negative message. By maintaining a more 'open' body position and using wider hand gestures rather than covering your mouth with your hand, you can instantly boost the way other people rate you.

Here's another big one that's simple to fix: posture. Leaders who command greater authority seldom slouch. They also rarely shift their feet nervously or play with their hands. The point of keeping all this in mind is not to get overwhelmed with a bunch of rules, but to raise the level of non-verbal awareness and slowly work on improving these skills throughout our careers.

If you have a quiet personality, or if you're still gaining proficiency in the language spoken in your office or city, non-verbal communication offers you a terrific opportunity. By mastering the art of 'saying something without saying anything'—the essence of non-verbal communication—you can maximize the interactions you have with your team members, customers or boss and leave them feeling like they've shared meaningful communication with you even if you only spoke a few words. And as your non-verbal soft skills improve, so will your verbal skills.

Know When to Speak Up and Avoid 'I . . . I . . . I . . . I'

One of the key concerns employees bring up with me is how they can make their presence felt. Maybe you go to a meeting, write some notes silently and leave. Then, afterwards, you say to yourself: Why didn't I speak up? Did I add value? Was I worried I might say something silly and embarrass myself? Another dimension to this concern is the issue of over-speaking.

> *'I believed the way to make an impression in a team meeting was to speak up constantly. Sometimes, I just made lots of unrelated points which weren't even useful.'*
>
> —Shivani (34), marketing professional, Chennai

Here's my advice to Shivani and countless others like her: Relax. Effective communication is not about putting on a show or speaking as many words as possible. It's about sharing authentic and meaningful ideas with other people. When I ask OYO's founder, Ritesh Agarwal, about this, he says authenticity is the essence of powerful communication. 'One thing to focus on in effective communication is authenticity. Authenticity is extremely critical in communication,' says Agarwal. When you view communication as a chance to build authentic connections, it takes so much pressure off. There's no need to feel like you should show off. Just focus on having a sincere exchange where you offer information and ideas to help the team.

First, pay attention to the active dialogue, and make notes where you want to add something, or put forward a different point of view and then pick the best time to speak up in a meeting, waiting for a natural pause in the dialogue. Then, start with something like, 'That's an interesting insight, because . . .' or 'Something you just said sparked an idea . . .' By structuring your interruption positively, you will lower any defensiveness or perception of rudeness before smoothly inserting your thought, question, or idea. Phrases like these also show others that you were listening and are adding value by building on what they just said.

Another way to build communicative bridges is to limit how often you use the word 'I'. Endlessly saying 'I . . . I . . . I . . . I . . . I' can irritate people and cause them to form early opinions or assume arrogance where there is none. Minimizing the use of 'I' also helps listeners focus on the core of your message, not the messenger.

Sometimes, people use 'we' instead of 'I' to try and sound less self-focused. 'We' is a great word, but there are some situations where you don't want use it. For example, if you are discussing a mistake that *you* made but instead say 'we', people will think you are trying to avoid responsibility. So when you need to be accountable for something you did, use 'I'. Saying 'I screwed up' sounds more direct and accountable than saying 'we'. Saying 'I take full responsibility' will earn you more respect. Also, if other team members feel accountable they'll take a cue from you and say, 'Yes, I too take responsibility', and then, just like that, you have taken the culture of your company to the next level. These easy-to-implement tips will go a long way towards strengthening your workplace communication if you are willing to practise and rehearse.

Write It Right

> *'Applying to jobs became a 24x7 activity for me, I would apply to ten jobs a day with the same cover letter and resume. In hindsight, my cookie-cutter approach and not focusing on smaller details and mistakes might have been the reason I wasn't succeeding.'*
>
> —Aakash (25), engineer, Pune

Aakash's resume was probably one of many received by the company. If you saw the mountains of resumes and applications that employers receive every week, you would be shocked. Cover letters riddled with spelling errors, resumes filled with grammatical mistakes, emails with poor punctuation, applications filled with generic answers that have obviously been copied and pasted over and over to multiple employers—employers see too much low-quality written communication in today's job market.

Now, think from the employer's perspective. If a person isn't even willing to spend the time and effort to write properly when *applying* for a job, just imagine the quality of their work when they are hired!

No one is saying you need to be a Shakespeare or a Tagore. But the care with which you write speaks volumes about you. Now, you may say, 'But, Ronnie, my peers and boss all send Slack, WhatsApp and email messages that are sloppy and messy. Why shouldn't I?'

Three reasons:

First, you want to set a higher standard for yourself professionally.

Second, over time, people who consistently communicate clearly and professionally move up and get considered for leadership roles.

And third, while you may have a colleague who uses slang, incomplete sentences and emojis to communicate with the boss, they may have other strengths that make the boss tolerate their poor communication skills. You never know.

Bottom line: write right. Reports, emails, project decks, PowerPoint presentations, even texts, all send a signal about the quality of your ideas and work ethic. We can all take an extra couple of minutes to review what we've written and give it a final polishing edit. Spell-check and grammar software are readily available. Use them.

Professionals who write properly stand out, land the job and get promoted.

5 Core Takeaways

- Employers seek and promote strong communicators. Regardless of the field you're in, refining your communication skills is a wise investment of time and energy.
- Organize your talking points and prepare and practise them whenever possible.
  Make sure you've adjusted your message for the group you're speaking to.
  Then, deliver your points and avoid over-talking.
- Just because you're not talking doesn't mean you're not communicating.
  Raising your level of non-verbal awareness will work wonders and strengthen your skills as a communicator. And don't forget eye contact.
- Use positive interjections more and the word 'I' less. These two techniques will help foster more meaningful connections with colleagues.
- The care with which you write or reply to emails or prepare your CV speaks volumes to your boss, colleague and company. Use proper spelling, punctuation and grammar. Doing so will set you apart and make you shine.

Call to Action

1. Be 'contagious'. I do want to be contagious in communication. Strong communication is meant

to spread and go viral. Strong communicators spread clarity and confidence. Be that. From today, start thinking, 'I am going to be contagious in my communication.'

2. Listening is one of the most important parts of communication (more on that in Chapter 5). Even while you're *learning* multiple ways in which to *up* your communication, switch *today* to being a great listener. It's the easiest thing to do, and by doing so you've already covered one-third of the path to being a great communicator.

2

Strive to Be a Storyteller

The first time I really understood the power of storytelling in a professional context was early in my career when I needed my first bank loan. Back then, getting a loan for a new business, however small, was very different. You had to go to a bank, meet the manager, have them review stacks of paperwork—it was almost like a job interview. On that day, I knew that unless I got that bank loan, my business wouldn't start and my ambitions would hit a wall.

When I arrived at the bank, the loan officer barely looked at me. I sat down and he said, 'So where are all your papers? Give me all your forms.' It was almost like I didn't need to be there—he was all business with virtually zero interaction. But this moment was too important to leave to chance. I absolutely *had* to get that loan. So I decided to attract his attention, stand out and make a lasting impression.

That's when I started telling him the 'story' of my business idea, how it came about, where I was when it started, and that I'd already interviewed and selected twenty people who were waiting for their job depending on this loan. At the start of my narration, he didn't seem too interested. But as I continued telling him the 'story' of my potential business and my plans, he looked up from the stack of papers, leaned forward, looked me in the eye and listened. I walked out of the bank with the loan sanctioned—and a lasting lesson about the power of applying work-related 'storytelling' during life-changing moments.

Stories are powerful because they influence and impact people by shaping minds and moving hearts. C.P. Gurnani summed it up this way: 'Storytelling is the secret sauce of communications. The words "Let me tell you a story . . ." are the five best words to start your presentation, pitch or conversation with.' I couldn't agree more. One of the reasons we all love stories is because they help us relate to one another. Learn. Grow. Build human connections with other people.

You have seen this in your own life. Someone shares a story about their childhood and it makes you smile. Or you tell a friend a funny story about something that happened over the weekend and it makes them sputter with laughter. Is there a better feeling than to evoke a powerful emotion in another? A story told well sparks a reaction. It captures attention. It leaves people with a memorable impression that sticks. Sanjeev Mehta tells me: 'If I have to reach the heart of a person then it has to be through a story. [Storytelling] helps improve data retention in the listener, enhances empathy and connectedness with whoever you're talking to, and most importantly, it primes the brain with new ideas when you lace facts and figures with a story.' I love Sanjeev's phrase that a great story 'primes the brain' to remember what's been said, because the power of storytelling is that it stays with listeners long after you're done speaking. Let me show you what I mean.

Imagine Akash and Karan, two people with similar educational degrees and work experience who go to a job interview for a data science position at a healthcare company. Both are asked the following question: 'Take two or three minutes and tell us about yourself. Also, why do you believe you are the right person for the job?' Akash does what most people do. He basically repeats what's already on his resume. He rambles on and on, repeating the details of each job, degree and internship on his resume until the interviewer is so bored she's ready to fall asleep.

Karan, however, takes a different approach. He says, 'I know you've reviewed my resume and already know my education and experience. But my interest in data science and healthcare actually began when I was a teenager and my aunt got sick and had to be rushed to the hospital . . .' He then tells a short and impactful story about how he later realized his aunt's health crisis could have been avoided through better digital health record-keeping and predictive computer modelling of her symptoms. He concludes his answer by saying, 'So, that early family experience really drives my passion for data science and how it can be used to save lives.'

Now, ask yourself. All other factors being equal, is it Akash or Karan who is likely to stand out? It's not even close. Karan, who told the story, is *far* more memorable and impactful. His story brings the speaker and listener closer together and lays bare things about him far beyond what any words could convey. That's the power of storytelling. It connects and helps people feel your passion and remember you in positive ways. It reminds me of Vijay Shekhar Sharma saying he learnt to use stories early on to overcome language and cultural barriers with potential funders. 'Stories give us a way to communicate how we are different, rather than just saying I am a different guy,' Vijay told me. 'I studied in a Hindi-medium school, but my engineering education was in English, so I had a *Taare Zameen Par* moment where alphabets were flying, lips were moving but I couldn't understand. So telling the story of my life in the early days and how I reached here made someone [potential funders] understand who I am, whether I am going to be a good guy to back or not.'

Bottom line: no matter what your work profile is, every task, strategy, idea or plan can have a story. Storytelling is a skill anyone can learn—and everyone must know.

How Do I Tell a Powerful Story?

Some people mistakenly believe that storytelling is a rare talent that only a small group of people are born with. Others think of storytelling narrowly, as only fancy PowerPoint presentations, or in terms of the many ways in which advertisers and marketers sell products. So what exactly is storytelling in a professional context? Put simply, it is the ability to explain a concept or an idea by connecting it to a story from your own life or observations.

Here's the good news: you are *already* a storyteller. You tell stories all the time in your personal life. Your friend or spouse asks, 'How was your day?' and you launch right into a story without giving it a second thought. It's natural. Humans are storytellers. So why should you hesitate about using storytelling at work? It is one of the skills achievers use to get ahead. Stories let others know you are clever, interesting, articulate and sincere. Vijay is a big believer in stories holding power far beyond words. 'Stories can communicate a lot more about yourself than your words will; stories bring sincerity and drive home the meaningfulness of your words.'

In other words, a strong storyteller is someone who knows how important it is to get the right kind of authentic attention and message across in a distracted world.

'Dhirubhai Ambani's story of how he came from nothing and became the biggest businessman in this country, that's a story worth hearing many times, but there is only one Dhirubhai, not everyone can have such a story to tell.'

—Nithya (24), MBA graduate, Kochi

When I hear Nithya's interpretation of storytelling, I immediately find it very limiting. The first step in telling a captivating story is believing that you have stories worth telling. You do. Your thoughts and experiences are what make you unique.

Don't sell yourself short. When you see a chance to tell a story to illustrate a key point, go for it! An easy way to start your story is to use a phrase like: 'What we're discussing right now reminds me of something that happened . . .' or 'What we're talking about is a little bit like . . .' Then tell your story and make your point.

To be clear: everything you communicate should not be a story. The power and impact of storytelling comes from selectively using it for those important moments when you want to make a strong impact. So you don't want to overuse storytelling. Harsh Goenka also notes that there are times when storytelling should not be used. 'Where storytelling does not work is when you have to give bad news,'

Goenka says. 'That's where you have to be proper and precise.' So, understand that the goal is not to be known as the office 'storyteller', but instead as the person who explains their points with power and impact by occasionally using a story or anecdote during an important moment to help people relate and connect to their message.

Remember: while people may forget what you say, they never forget how you made them feel. And that's the power of storytelling. It helps people experience feelings and ideas that they can't otherwise see. When I ask Apollo Hospitals CEO Suneeta Reddy about professional storytelling, she says, 'I can't just *tell* people nothing is impossible, it doesn't make sense. I have to *show* them, and a story helps prove to them that nothing is impossible.' So let's learn how easy and fun storytelling can be.

Keep It Short and Simple

The best and most effective stories are short and simple. For example, I try to keep mine to no more than a minute or two. Any longer than that and you risk losing people's attention. Or worse, listeners get so lost in your story they miss the point you are making.

> *'Consider every conversation like a sales pitch. Go in with two clear ideas to convey. Don't overdo it, convey them in a precise manner and walk away.'*
>
> —Rama (28), IT professional, Bangalore

I like the practicality in Rama's thought process. Remember, the goal of a story is to drive home a point or to take a complex idea and make it simple. The clearer your story, the better you will communicate your point.

Several years ago, my team and I were stuck on an execution plan. After two long meetings over seven days—where we debated for hours on the best way to proceed on a project—no one was willing to make any final decisions. I could have taken the call, but I needed it to be a team decision and for them to own it. I realized I needed to shake things up and push my team forward. So, I told them the following story:

> What we're experiencing right now reminds me of something that happened to me when I was eight years old. My dad had taken me to the club (CCI) so I could learn to swim. The swimming instructor did

> his best to teach me, but I just couldn't get the hang of it and I never left the shallow side of the pool.
>
> Then, suddenly, my dad picked me up and tossed me into the deep end of the pool. No floats, nothing. I went down and came up . . . down and up, again. Was I scared? Of course! But after a few seconds, I managed to surface and stay afloat, much to my father's delight. Problem solved. From then on, I swam. Life is a little like that. At some point, we just have to jump in, take the plunge and figure out how to 'swim'.

Do you see how that works? The story is short, simple, clear and makes a point people are likely to remember. Moreover, as Amitabh Kant says, one should feel free to add 'a bit of soul, a bit of punch, a bit of drama, a little humour' when crafting one's story. Once you get the hang of it, it's quite fun. Read my Call to Action points at the end of this chapter and try it for yourself.

Don't Exaggerate and Be Consistent

Sometimes, people confuse storytelling with wild exaggeration, lying or stretching the truth just to entertain or be different. Don't do that. Effective storytelling is not making things up. It's sharing a true experience with people to make a point. (In the example I used above, my father really did throw me into the deep end of the pool when I was eight years old.) Telling true stories builds trust. People are smart. They can tell when someone is full of BS. Don't go there. There's no need to. When I discuss what to avoid when using storytelling, OYO's

Ritesh Agarwal emphasizes, 'There is a fundamental difference between storytelling and spinning,' he says. 'I believe spinning is wrong in any situation, but storytelling to me is another form of strong communication.'

> *'Sometimes, I get too excited and add in some harmless spicy details that make a story even more interesting. But later on, it's tough to remember the details.'*
>
> —Nitin Kamath (36), product manager, Nagpur

While Nitin's habit might seem harmless, it could lead to trouble because people will notice inconsistencies or contradictions when he retells the same story in different ways. This is the other reason I think you should avoid the BS factor. It's needlessly stressful. Everyone will have a smile on their face, and you may think you've got them captivated by your story, but inside they're thinking: *This guy is full of BS! Last month he told this same story on Instagram but it was totally different. What a liar!* Tell a true story and retell it consistently, and you'll have no problems.

Incorporate Storytelling into Your Daily Routine

Since learning is no longer a one-time event, you should approach storytelling as a lifelong skill that you will practise and improve for years to come. In fact, as Harsh Goenka notes, many leading companies are now making storytelling a key area of leadership training for those looking to move up. 'Storytelling is especially important when you're addressing a large group. For example, we in RPG have formal storytelling classes for our top brass; we found that extremely useful and now we're taking it to the next level.'

Even if your company doesn't offer such training, there are opportunities to discover new anecdotes every waking moment. Keep your ears and eyes open. Push yourself to collect personal stories and see how you can use them to illustrate an important idea in your work. Before you know it, you will begin to view the world around you in exciting and creative ways. Vani Kola says one simple way to learn storytelling is to 'try telling your stories to kids in your family' because given children's honest nature, 'you'll know where you're flat or where you're effective or not'. Another creative way to integrate stories in everyday life is shown in Harsh's story below.

'When my seniors from abroad visit, I won't just tell them about the best places in Delhi, I'll show them around post-work, and tell them my personal stories about each place. If you wish to sell your product to a client, don't tell them why it's better than the competitor's, focus on making them experience it. The same applies here.'

—Harsh (30), trading professional, Delhi

You will also benefit by watching others tell stories. A great resource to see the power of effective storytelling in a professional context is TED Talks. Regardless of whether your career is in big data, business management, machine learning, law, digital marketing or insurance, there are TED Talks by experts on almost every topic. TED Talks take many, many hours to prepare. These speakers have to create dazzling, original speeches to a very wide group—all over ten to eighteen minutes. Pay attention to how the best speakers use stories to explain their ideas or simplify complex concepts. Then work to develop and polish your own storytelling skills. I'll tell you what's worked for me. Observing. I am always on the lookout to hear how anyone opens up and tells their stories. It's happening around you all the time. Just be open to listening.

5 Core Takeaways

- You have a story to tell. Many stories, in fact. Don't sell yourself short. Speak up!
- Telling a captivating story helps people remember you and your ideas. Use them when you want to explain or emphasize an important point.
- An easy way to start is to say, 'What we're discussing right now reminds me of something that happened . . .' or 'What we're talking about is a little bit like . . .' Remember, the goal is to connect to the idea you're communicating to make it memorable and meaningful.
- The most effective stories are simple, short, clear and true. Don't tell lies or use wild exaggeration. People know BS when they hear it.
- Storytelling opens up a new world of creativity and possibilities. Pay attention to your daily experiences and consider how they might make powerful stories. Watching other professionals do the same will trigger new ideas.

Call to Action

1. Write down experiences in your life that impacted or influenced you the most. Think of the times when you felt most elated or when you were down and write out those thoughts—turn them into anecdotes or stories as that will show the real you. Make your personality come alive by sharing your stories.
2. Now that you understand the power of storytelling, find out other people's stories. Get your colleagues and your boss to open up to you, use this to bond with them, and understand them better by listening to their stories.

3

You Don't Have to Be Big to Think Big

There are dozens of excuses not to think big. Dump all of them in the dustbin. As Sanjeev Mehta puts it, 'It's not about the deck of cards you're served, it's about what you do with them.'

So you didn't score high in school or graduate at the top of your class. Big deal.

I *failed* my second year of college. No joke. When it happened, my first thought was that my life was over. Done. Finished. I would forever be haunted by a red-inked resume—one that told the world I was such a failure that I couldn't even make it through my second year of college. Worse, I feared I had failed my parents. They had worked and saved their hard-earned money for years just so I could go to school. Now, I was worried I had brought them disappointment and shame.

Then, I took a breath, calmed down, and pushed away the initial cloud of fear. My parents were upset and disappointed, but I used their saddened reaction as fuel to get myself focused. I then took the failed subjects again, finished with strong marks, and kept going. It was a powerful lesson in humility. From then on, I worked hard and never took things for granted.

You don't have any money to pursue your goals? I can relate to that. When I was eighteen years old, I was faced with my first big financial loss. I did not have any money to my name prior to that anyway, but I was broke. Two of my friends and I decided to host a rock concert. It was a great show but commercially it was a flop. We were 50,000 rupees in loss—an enormous amount to us at that point in life. It took me almost a *year* to first beg and borrow and then pay it back. But I did. Today, I consider that one of my important early lessons.

You come from a small town? So what? Who cares? Perhaps you care, but guess who does not? Me and numerous CEOs, leaders, founders and corporate employers. How do I know? Because I asked them for you. In fact, many of them told me coming from a small town is actually an *advantage*, not a negative. Here's how Vijay Shekhar Sharma explains it: 'Coming from a small town gives you extra ammunition—that you are not ashamed of trying something, you are not ashamed of anything that doesn't work, you are open to any possibility. When you come from a small town, your success parameters are small, which means you have more successes in life.' Vijay isn't alone in his thinking; Harsh Goenka agrees. 'When I interview a person, and I see a person who is from a city and a person from a small village and they both have the same CV, I always choose the one from the smaller place, because he brings in a lot of hard work and he has the necessary hunger.'

And if all that hasn't convinced you, OYO's Ritesh Agarwal is quick to point out, 'India has so many stories of people like our Prime Minister Narendra Modi, who started out small.'

Vijay, Harsh and Ritesh are obviously 100 per cent spot on. And besides, in India, there is no such thing as a *small* town, because 'small' can actually have some *big* advantages. So don't let anyone make you feel 'less' for *any* reason. Ever.

Oh, you didn't go to a fancy school? If you're a high-growth problem-solver, where you went to school is not nearly as important as you think it is. It just isn't. My first school was Dunne's Institute, Mumbai. I'm very proud of that school, but it wasn't known for English language fluency, or for anything else for that matter. Around 95 per cent of the students came to school by public transport, including me. At a much later stage, my parents moved me to another school in south Bombay, and I was proud of that one too. But suddenly, I realized that 90 per cent of the kids at that school arrived in cars, while I used to travel by bus. I didn't let that rattle my confidence. My friends at the new school had pocket money, which I didn't. They would want to go to eat at a restaurant, but I didn't have any money. They were nice enough to pay for my food, and I returned the kindness by bringing my buddies delicious home-cooked Parsi food, which they all liked.

Success does not pay attention to which city you come from or went to. What success *does* pay attention to is whether you are a problem-solver who works hard for the team and adds value. When I speak with Kiran Mazumdar-Shaw, she makes it crystal clear what matters most: 'If there is a question, or there is a problem to be solved and if I ask people to solve a problem, I want to know how clear is their thought process of solving that problem. That's very important to me. I just don't discriminate on the basis of which part of the country they came from.'

Kiran's view is shared widely. It doesn't matter where you start in life; only where you finish. So it's time to learn to let your fears melt away. If you think small, you will be small. If you think big, you will become big. Stop worrying and start aiming higher.

I have lived that life. Coming from a lower-middle-class family, but living in a city like Mumbai, which is the commercial capital of India, can make a lot of demands and put pressures on you. Did that scare me at the start? Of course it did. But I did not let that lower my self-esteem. In fact, my desire to build my self-confidence and self-conviction only became stronger.

Face and Crush Your Fears

The first step in learning how to think big is facing your fears. We all have them.

For example, many people fear disappointing their parents. For others, it is a fear of falling short in comparison to one's peers. Whatever the source, it all boils down to a general fear of failure that is often about not being good enough in the eyes of others—a flawed idea in the first place. When that happens, pressure and stress pile up like a wall of bricks that separates us from our deepest ambitions. What you need to understand is that first comes fear, then failure. And every time you fail, your fear goes down, and then one fine day it's not there. So if you sit on the fence for life, worried and fearful of failure, you're stuck for life. Better to get the failures we all must experience out of the way, and let fear melt away to make way for you to pursue your personal ambitions. Let's be clear—you have hopes and goals, whether you realize it or not. The biggest tragedy is when a person's ambitions get buried under stress and pressure.

> *'My older brother cracked his CA exams early, I have been trying since years but am stuck. What if I am not meant to be a CA? I am too afraid to think of what else to do with my life.'*
>
> —Nikita (29), CA aspirant, Bhopal

Nikita's dilemma isn't unique to her; I am sure many of you have felt similar fear in your life too. To her I'll say, Nikita, I failed my second year in college. My first reaction was—maybe I was not cut out for academics (and I was right), but at that moment I had to prove to myself that I could fix this and then move on. Yours is a tough exam. You have to figure out what's important to you at that time and then action it. So, what can you do to smash the wall of fear and think big? Answer: create a new mindset about failure. There's a famous saying that the word fear stands for **F**-alse, **E**-vidence, **A**-ppearing, **R**-eal. It means that the things we're afraid of are often not rooted in reality. That's a good starting point, but it doesn't go far enough. The key is learning to *embrace* failure as a natural, normal and even beneficial part of work. I've failed *far* more than I've succeeded in everything I've done. Everyone experiences failures. They keep you grounded and teach you to stay at it and keep going.

Start by eliminating this toxic question from your mind: What will happen if I fail? The minute you start down that mental road is the minute pressure and stress come roaring back into your mind. So reframe the question: What will happen if I allow myself to try? Notice I didn't ask what will happen if I 'succeed'. There's no way to know what will happen. But that's not the point. By *allowing yourself to try*, there will be beneficial outcomes, regardless. Nikita tried hard. Maybe she will get through on her next attempt, maybe she will realize or decide she has another calling. Maybe she needs to stop comparing herself with her brother! Has she failed? Not at all. Will the setback teach her strong life lessons and give her more clarity on what she really wants to do? Absolutely. She will learn. Gain new insights. Evolve.

Bottom line: fear is the enemy of thinking big. Confront and crush it.

You Have the Right to Think Big

When we are young and starting out in our careers, we sometimes lack the self-confidence or sense of self-worth required to think big. When a person says they don't have any major goals, it is often because they do not believe they deserve to think big and have major goals. Maybe kids made fun of them in school (as it happens to most of us growing up). Perhaps a teacher or parent treated them harshly. Or maybe they grew up in a family where they had to put everyone else's needs above their own and therefore felt uncomfortable or 'selfish' thinking about their own wishes and desires.

> *'When you come from IIM, MDI or FMS, that's when employers welcome your resume. Does schooling from a government school and college from a small private college bring one a realistic right to dream for the moon?'*
> —Omar (24), sales professional, Greater Noida

The answer to Omar's concern is simple: Everyone has the right to think big. Don't sell yourself short. Give yourself permission to think big. *You* determine the shape and size of your goals. They change with age. Marriage and children, home ownership, educational goals, financial investing, starting a business, learning a new skill or hobby, political aspirations, job promotions, health and fitness, spiritual or charity goals and now #LifeLongLearning—there is a world of possibilities to explore.

Take the Driver's Seat

There's no escaping the fact that the way we were raised colours the way we see our life and work. We carry into adulthood both the wonder and magic of childhood as well as the scars and difficulties. Most parents and families do their best to raise their children with love, support and guidance. Tragically, some of us experience trauma, neglect or worse. But whatever your background, know this: while the past can affect the future, it does not determine it. That means regardless of past experiences—positive or negative—adult achievements depend entirely on what one does right now.

> *'I moved to Mumbai six months ago from Jodhpur. I have to work, but my parents want me to tell them everything, from when I get to work to when I get back home, and to not travel after dark. Between juggling my parents and this new city, I don't know what I am even doing at work.'*
>
> —Priya (25), junior analyst, Mumbai

To feel overwhelmed in a new environment like Priya does is normal, but you need to take control of your life as quickly as possible. Otherwise, you get so used to mom or dad doing things for you that you lose the ability to think and act for yourself.

Worse, you begin to actually *enjoy* the feeling of not making decisions. Put simply, you are 'outsourcing' personal responsibility and decision-making to others. Then, when the time comes to break free and stand on your own two feet, you feel stressed out. Alone. Lost.

Another important factor in thinking big is not to base your ambitions on a desire to impress others. Instead, focus your work and energy on doing what you love. I recognize that in the early part of a person's career (the first five to ten years) it can take some time to figure out the work you're most passionate about. It is also true that our present education system is not set up to allow us to take multiple and varied college courses that can help us find out what we're most interested in. But until those things are fixed, we must do it for ourselves.

It's your life. So live it. Get in the driver's seat, grip the steering wheel, and learn to drive through life on your own. The sooner you do that, the sooner you can begin your journey and reach the destination of your own choosing. But first, say this to yourself even louder than any 'Om' chant you do in the mornings. 'It's my life and I'm in control.' The problem is many of us don't actually want to be in the driver's seat. We've led such protected lives thanks to our parents and family that we are not really sure of our own destination. We are more than happy for others to take decisions for us. We look for someone else to push us, and before we know it we become so dependent on everyone and everything that we hardly have our own self-confidence or clarity. This is the right place to be. Scream, 'It's my life.'

The Comfort Zone Kills Big Thinking

If you are comfortable, your goals are doomed.

Read the above sentence again. Then say it to yourself. Every. Single. Day.

Thinking big does not happen inside the 'comfort zone'. Big ideas force us to stretch beyond our current abilities. That's why slipping into the lazy comfort zone is so dangerous. If you do, you will start saying things to yourself like, *I got my degree. I'm done learning. I have a job and just need to get by. There's no need to excel or stand out. Just do the work, stay quiet, go unnoticed and get paid.* Maybe your parents were in jobs—government jobs or others—where there was a sense of job security and stability. Those days are gone. Forever. Just look at the speed of global disruption, uncertainty and job losses caused by the pandemic.

> *'I just want my salary increments to be such that I can live with ease, that's my dream. If I didn't get a salary for three months, I would struggle to meet some of my family expenses. My goal is to keep getting a regular salary hike and be steady.'*
>
> —Ramit (35), father of two, Gurgaon

Ramit's concerns are fair, but is his plan foolproof? I don't think so, because the way to future-proof yourself against getting crushed by the speed of global change is to pursue lifelong learning. First, admit to yourself that what you studied or learned five years back already seems less relevant. Understand that just learning on the job is not going to be enough, because the most you can learn on the job is how to do the same things better. But the world is not looking for people who can do something incrementally better. It's time to urgently figure out not where 'your' career is going, but what the careers of tomorrow are. It may be time to get off one train, wait on the platform just long enough to know what and how your new learning starts and board that train to a journey of lifelong learning. That will set in motion a constant cycle of new growth, creativity and skills that will keep your abilities fresh and relevant. That's the secret recipe for thinking big.

Perhaps you're thinking: *What happens if I go after my goals and can't reach them?* My answer is a quote from the legendary advertising pioneer Leo Burnett, who said, 'When you reach for the stars you may not quite get one, but you won't come up with a handful of mud either.' In other words, good things happen to those who think big, regardless of the outcome.

Write It Down

There is power in writing things down. Writing turns the thoughts in your mind into something you can see and hold.

> *'I want to be in Forbes 30 under 30, but my family tells me, and I also know, that it's just a silly dream. I am not doing anything unique in my life, so getting there will be a miracle.'*
>
> —Fauzia (23), BPO worker, Hyderabad

Dear Fauzia, do this: Take out a piece of a paper. Draw a vertical line down the middle of the page. Call the left column '12-month Goals' and the right side '5- to 10-year Goals'. Then list your ambitions under each category. Don't hold back; no one else is going to see this. Write down everything. If you catch yourself hesitating to write something, that's fear trying to hold you back—so push past it and write it down.

Next, commit to doing at least two things every week to inch closer to achieving your short- and long-range ambitions. For example, if one of your lifelong learning goals is to get your pilot's licence and learn to fly an airplane, read an aviation article or watch a tutorial video weekly. Maybe it's not flying. Perhaps it's investing in stocks, learning a new language, starting a new business, buying a home—it doesn't matter. You can do two things each week—or daily, to get quicker results—to achieve your ambitions. Look at your list every Sunday night to reset and refocus your brain. Then, attack the week, fuelled by big thinking.

I don't want you to stop doing this exercise, of writing things down—committing to two things at a time, reviewing them and writing them down. Keep this list safely. It's one of the most important notes to keep looking back on as you move on in your career. So much more becomes a priority when you write it down. If you keep notes and a report card you can read a year later, it can also be a career tracker.

5 Core Takeaways

- Confront and smash your fears early on. Once you do, you will discover your hidden ambitions.
- Give yourself permission to think big. Your self-worth and self-confidence depend on it. The sooner you take charge of your own life and do things for yourself, the better.
- If you're 'comfortable', you're doomed. Lifelong learning isn't a buzz phrase; it's the new global reality. Thinking big always forces you to live outside your comfort zone.
- Respect your goals enough to write them down—both short-term and long-range.

- Resolve to do two things weekly to inch you closer to achieving them over time.

Call to Action

1. Most of us obsess about being someone else, and then we set that person as the benchmark and strive to be her/him, not realizing that what we see is never what we get, and that the other person also has many other dimensions. Whenever I've tried to be someone else and focused only on competing with them or doing better than them, I have failed. This is partly because I'm so busy looking over my shoulder rather than looking forward, and partly because real success is when I compete with who I was yesterday and keep improving. Individual growth is a treadmill and you need to be really honest with yourself. If you are, you are guaranteeing real growth for yourself.
2. The secret of winning as a manager, boss or leader is by making your team win. Leaders never win on their own. They ensure they make their team win. So remember this next time you push for a team member's performance or focus on their flaws—your job is to make them grow and win. Your road from manager to CEO would be much smoother if you get this right eight times out of ten.

4

All Shine, No Whine

Spend enough time at a corporate or start-up and you will observe that those who advance the most often complain the least—even when they have a legitimate reason to do so. I've found that this principle holds true among top talent in other industries as well. Achievers are too busy shining to waste time whining.

Case in point: Shah Rukh Khan. It was 2003, and we were shooting the film *Swades*, one of my favourite movie productions, and later eponymous with our Swades Foundation. In the movie, Shah Rukh plays a NASA engineer and Ivy League graduate in the US who returns to his home in rural India when his parents die. The longer he remains in India, the more he longs to stay and bring change.

The main location for the film was a place called Wai, situated at the foothills of Panchgani and Mahabaleshwar in Maharashtra. One scene required Shah Rukh's character to visit a rustic hut near the mountains. To film the scene, we had to make a brutal three-hour journey through some of the most treacherous terrain I've ever seen. For weeks, Shah Rukh had suffered serious back problems that were so severe that doctors were discussing surgery to be done immediately after we finished the movie. With every jolt and bump we hit along the ride, I could see Shah Rukh's face clench in pain. When we finally arrived at the location, we realized the tiny hut could have easily been built on a studio set—the immensely painful three-hour ride could have been avoided.

Many A-list movie stars in that situation would have thrown a tantrum. Demanded VIP treatment. Exploded in an entitled rage. Shah Rukh did none of that. He acknowledged the situation and didn't say another word about it before turning in a world-class performance. There's a reason we call him 'Sleepless Shah Rukh'—he gives his all and never quits. All shine, no whine.

Reject the Entitled Mindset

Sometime during our teenage years, we realize one of life's realities: no one really owes us anything. Not a job, not a career, not a promotion, nothing. That's just the way the world works. We then go off to college, get our first job, and—bam!—once again we're reminded that our career advancement, professional development, promotions and salary raises all depend on our actions, ambition and determination to add value. At first, hitting that wall of reality can feel like too much rests only on your shoulders. But it's important to remember that asking for help is never a weakness. Nor is it a sign of incompetence. Sometimes, the challenges one faces are large and complex, and therefore you need your team members to step in and offer guidance. That's okay. No one expects you to be superhuman. So, understand that teamwork is the mark of any great company.

The challenge comes when we begin to shift the normal stresses that come with any job on to others. Your colleagues and your boss expect you to be clear about your role, task or job and execute on it. Many times, we look sideways before we execute, looking for support, checking if others are on the job, leaning on others to get going. Be a self-starter. Take control. That's a problem that can lead to a lack of personal responsibility and self-awareness.

'I feel I don't get proper recognition at work, and the higher authorities just put the responsibilities on someone else's shoulder and don't take accountability for not mentoring us fully.'

—Mangal (26), equity researcher, Bangalore

Mangal may be right in saying that his company could do more. However, professionals who get ahead reject what's known as the entitlement mindset. The word 'entitlement' is defined as 'the belief that one is inherently deserving of privileges and special treatment'. The reason employers find this attitude so offensive is because it's not team-oriented. In essence, an entitled employee is saying, *I'm more important than others and therefore deserve better treatment and advantages than the rest of the team.* Few things are more toxic to teamwork than someone who demands special treatment, complains constantly, or blames their errors on others. All that negative energy is unhelpful. Vijay Shekhar Sharma says that professionals who rise choose a different approach. 'There are two kinds of employees and two kinds of teammates in every team: ones who always see what's wrong, and ones who always see hope—let's fix it and get it done. The world progresses through people with hope and action,' Sharma says.

Vijay is right. Regardless of how high up you are in your company, always do your best to have a positive outlook and treat every person with equal respect and consideration. I love how C.P. Gurnani puts it: 'Every time you whine is a waste of sixty seconds that you can use to polish yourself and shine (again).' Better to focus one's time on shining than whining.

Your Career Is Your Responsibility

Every large company has a few negative people who complain about . . . well, almost everything. These individuals are easy to spot. They criticize their colleagues, boss, company and anyone else they can think of—on smoke breaks, at the water cooler, over lunch and when they get home. It's unfortunate. Imagine how much they might accomplish if they applied all that time to positive problem-solving!

Being a lifelong learner means taking control of your own professional growth.

Thankfully, many companies offer a lot of direct and indirect training. If your employer offers professional development opportunities to enhance your skills and knowledge, take advantage of them. If you work in a larger corporation and are new, you may not even know about some of the professional development options available to you. Ask your colleagues or human resources department. Sometimes there are informal training sessions, boot camps or brainstorm groups. Take time to bond and connect with peers, particularly in group gatherings. Starting a first or second job can be lonely; try to get out of your shell and not be a loner. Find buddies who can be a source of support through bad days and good. These are often the people who can also inform you of additional resources that may be available to you.

> *'There is a lack of opportunity and freedom to develop creatively and further our skillset. We are all just another pair of hands to do a job.'*
>
> —Lavanya (34), advertising professional, Mumbai

As for people like Lavanya, who work at places with fewer organizational opportunities for personal development, don't let that stop you from improving on your own. Instead of saying, 'What my boss/company should do to make me a better employee is . . .', say, 'What *I* can do to make myself a better employee is . . .' The difference between those two sentences is the difference between those who fall behind and those who zoom ahead. The first sentence says, *It is the company's responsibility to improve my career*. The second sentence says, *It is* MY *responsibility to improve my career*. Employers want self-motivated professionals. The faster you take control of your career trajectory, the faster you will rise.

Raise Your Level of Self-Awareness

Well, let's face it: You can't take credit for victories if you won't accept responsibility for mistakes.

Self-awareness means being honest about when you are at your best, as well as acknowledging when you could have done better. Early in our careers, we often obsess over not 'messing up' or making a mistake. (The irony, of course, is that a junior person's mistakes are more easily forgiven than a senior person's.) But you cannot claim credit for a win if you never accept responsibility for a loss. This is especially true for team projects. You are always going to win some and fail some, and you can only take credit for success if you are also leading from the front when there is a failure.

> *'We were a team of twenty-three- to twenty-five-year-olds, and our manager was quite friendly with us. Once we fell short of meeting our deadline, we took it too easy and it was our collective bad. But she rose to the occasion and took the fall, both with the senior management and with us. She explained how it was on her to ensure we do our work.'*
>
> —Amogh (30), operations lead, Chennai

Amogh was fortunate to have a boss with a strong sense of personal responsibility. But have you noticed how some people are quick to take all the credit when their team succeeds, but none of the blame when the team fails? Employers notice that, too. In fact, one thing that stands out most positively is when a person on the team who was actually one of the *strongest* members steps up and accepts their share of responsibility for the team not hitting the mark. That's an emerging leader. Wherever Amogh's boss is now, I'm sure she is an excellent team leader.

Teamwork is important, but not easy. None of us can be the best at every role or specialty. That's the greatest part of teamwork: it makes everyone look good and benefits all.

Work to Shine

A lot has been written about younger professionals—in their late teens or early twenties—much of it negative.

Critics say that today's 'Instagram Generation' is self-absorbed and lazy. I think that is a grossly unfair generalization. Still, it is true that social media and the way we express ourselves on it has changed the way we view ourselves. In some cases, it has created a misplaced level of overconfidence bordering on arrogance. Moreover, social media has encouraged people to fall in love with the sound of their own tweets, rather than letting hard and brilliant work speak for itself. My advice: be a grinder, someone who works harder than she talks. Mediocrity doesn't cut it. Besides, who wants to be mediocre? Work to shine.

The lower a person's level of entitlement, the more their work stands out. Why?

Because an entitled worker thinks: *I don't need to work as hard to get to the top. I'm smarter than people who have worked here for years.* But just because they may be smarter or more exposed to things globally than older employees, it doesn't mean they have the experience, awareness, maturity or knowledge of how to react in a crisis. As time passes, entitled people eventually hit the wall of reality and start worrying, *Why am I not getting ahead? I'm smarter and better! What happened?!*

> *'If I want a certain lifestyle in ten years then I am the only one who can work towards living it and earning for it. I need to keep my eyes and ears open for opportunities, always.'*
>
> —Sharmishtha (23), MBA graduate, Kolkata

I like Sharmishtha's spirit; in fact, not just me but all employers do. Vijay Shekhar Sharma shares with me that one of the core traits of those who rise to the manager or CEO level can be seen in individuals who create solution-focused plans and maintain a positive, can-do outlook. 'In life, and in a company, you will always move that one person to the top who sees possibility in every situation,' Sharma continues. 'If you're telling me what's wrong, you're not telling me something new, I already know that—so when a new CEO or manager is brought into a company, if she/he can say this is wrong, that is wrong, they are not going to be recruited because they know only what is wrong; that does not mean she/he is going to be able to do anything about it. I want a person with a plan. You don't vote for a leader in an election who says our country is in the gutter. You vote for someone who says we will build it together.'

Vijay is right. Employers promote and reward talented employees who are humble, confident and hard-working. Be that person.

3 Magic Words Self-Reliant Pros Use

> *'In India, decisions are made for you, from what you'll study to who you'll marry. It took me ten years to realize all my professional decisions are taken by my manager and I have never exercised any real say in anything.'*
>
> —Akshay (33), senior software developer, Pune

Akshay's story is sad but true. However, here's the exciting part: the more personal responsibility you take, the more your employer will trust you with decision-making power. As employers see you take ownership of your work, they will give you bigger and more important decisions and projects. Why? Because bosses understand that a person who can't make small decisions for themselves cannot be trusted to make big decisions for the company.

So how can you alert your team members, manager or CEO that you are ready and able to take on greater tasks? Self-reliant professionals use three magic words to let their managers and colleagues know they have the drive and confidence to tackle bigger responsibilities. Here they are: 'I'll handle it.'

When you tell your boss or team members, 'I'll handle it', you're communicating many things all at once. In effect, you are saying to others: *Don't worry. I will solve this problem and manage it to completion. You can trust me. I take responsibility for solving this problem, which also means I will have earned the right to get the credit once I've handled it. Consider this headache solved. I've got this.* Whether you are an engineer, lawyer, business analyst, digital marketer or data scientist, all employers love a decisive problem-solver—someone who overcomes challenges without having to be spoon-fed.

The next time your boss mentions a problem—small or large—tell them,

'I'll handle it.' Then, take care of the issue like you promised you would. The job responsibilities and decision-making power you will gain moving forward will grow exponentially over time.

5 Core Takeaways

- An entitled mindset is toxic and not team-focused. Reject it.
- Your career and professional growth are your responsibility. Always ask yourself, 'What can *I* do to make myself a better employee, team member, colleague and add value to my job and career?'
- Increasing self-awareness will strengthen your level of personal responsibility and avoid apportioning blame.
- 'Good enough' never is. You're better than mediocre. Work to shine.
- Use the three magic words, 'I'll handle it.' Then watch your decision-making authority and work responsibilities climb over time.

Call to Action

1. Repeat to yourself every day, 'I am not a failure until the day I start blaming others and everything around me.'
2. Remember, it's always the 'fear' factor never the 'failure' factor. So easy to say, but how does one get over fear of failure? Well, you have no choice. Think of it this way:
   a. 'Failure is never permanent.' Say that to yourself ten times a day.
   b. Just go out and do it—the thing you're most scared of. What's the worst that will happen? You'll be surprised, and the fear will start to go away.

5

The New LOL: Listen, Observe, Learn

One of my worst habits used to be interrupting people and not letting them finish speaking. I thought I was being super smart by cutting people off before they were done speaking. 'Look, I got it. I got it,' I'd say abruptly in the middle of their sentence. Not only was it rude, it was also just plain wrong. There was no possible way for me to read their mind and know exactly what they might say next. Then my mom said something I've never forgotten since.

One day she said to me, 'Ronnie, when the food comes to the table, do you start putting chillies and salt in your food before even tasting it? Would you do that?' And I told her, 'No, obviously not. I have to taste the food, figure out if it lacks salt or spice and then I can put things in.' She smiled and said, 'So why don't you listen and let people finish? Just like you don't know if your food needs salt or spices, you don't know what the other person's thoughts and ideas are unless you listen and don't interrupt.' Wise woman, my mom.

Listening is a skill I've worked very hard to improve throughout my career. And notice that I said *listening*, not hearing. There is a huge difference. Hearing just means soundwaves enter your ears. Listening requires much more. It demands focused thought, attention to detail, feedback and the ability to absorb words to decode what a person is *really* saying.

Listen, Observe, Learn—that's the new LOL, without which you will be DOA! Listening and acting on feedback from others helps us avoid repeating mistakes and accelerates professional growth and change. Vijay Shekhar Sharma explains the process this way: 'There is no way the other person will have a buy-in unless the one who is speaking has been heard completely. The fact that we want to align, make someone listen and follow what we say starts with us first listening and bringing that person's guard down, because now he is going to listen. So the sequence of change is that you listen, you understand, and then you speak. This is the only way you can appreciate a great idea, or actually make a team align to a single purpose.'

Think about how powerful what Vijay is saying really is. Through effective listening, you can motivate and unite your team. Let's take a deeper look at the finer points of effective listening and learn how to do it.

Eliminate Distractions

Confession: I am so distracted by people who stare at their screens instead of actively listening during a meeting that I confiscate phones. Think I'm joking? Ask my team members.

Before an important meeting, I have my executive assistant enter the room, announce that we offer a free, full-service 'mobile valet', gather up all phones and promise everyone that their beloved devices will be safe and secure until after the meeting. It's a fun way of removing a serious obstacle to attentive listening. 'Many times you're hearing and not listening, because your biggest enemy is your mobile,' explains Harsh Goenka. I obviously agree, which is why I snatch people's phones away before a meeting!

But even if you don't go that far, understand that the biggest threat to effective listening and observation is distraction. The next time you're in a meeting, look around the room. Notice how many people are scrolling through messages on their phones. Or tapping away on their laptops, answering emails while pretending they are 'taking notes'. (If you are truly taking notes on your laptop, then that's fine. But we all know that's not always the case.) I don't know about you, but I find that it takes me a full five minutes to bring my focus back to what I'm doing once I've been distracted. And five minutes can be a long time to be 'switched off' mentally from those around you.

> *'When other people would talk in a meeting and it didn't relate to me, I would only be thinking of my next key point or my pending tasks for the day as opposed to listening to their viewpoint.'*
>
> —Ranjan (25), engineer, Coimbatore

Ranjan realized his behaviour was a shortcoming, but many people justify such behaviour as a form of 'multitasking' (more on that later in the multitasking chapter). But it's not. It's rude. It also weakens one's ability to listen and absorb information. When people take time out of their day to meet you, it is impolite not to give them your full attention and focus.

This applies to bosses as well. In fact, I would say one of the worst examples a leader can set for their team is being distracted or answering texts when they have ten team members sitting right in front of them. If your boss has this bad habit, don't adopt it. You may think to yourself: *If he does it so can I . . . It's just the way we do things in this company*. Resist the urge to think that way. Instead, set a higher standard as you climb the ranks of managerial leadership.

Another form of distracted listening happens when a person switches off their brain during the parts of a meeting that do not directly deal with them. They say to themselves, *I've said my ten minutes about sales and marketing, so now I can tune out while the coders and IT people ramble on about tech implementation*. Viewing listening in such purely transactional terms (thinking you can ignore what doesn't concern you) is an amateur mistake. Why? Because it's a missed opportunity to learn, absorb and discover new points of connection between your area of specialty and the other parts of your company's business.

If nothing else, actively listening to your colleagues will increase the odds they will return the favour and actively listen to you. The first step is to get rid of distractions. So put the phone down. And as for the laptop, be true to yourself about whether you are truly taking notes or simply being distracted answering emails, etc.

Once you give colleagues the courtesy of your full focus, you're on your way to unlocking the full power of listening.

Listen to Absorb, Not Just React

Now that you've eliminated distractions, the next step is to develop the mindset of a strong listener. Workplace listening typically involves taking in feedback from one's boss, managers and most importantly your co-workers (the people who are closest to the work you do each day).

> *'I kept reaching out to everyone, and it felt like there was no way for me to understand my errors. Analysis was the core of my work, if no one looked it over, how would I move forward?'*
>
> —Vandana (27), coder, Chandigarh

Let's evaluate Vandana's situation in further detail. In the first year or so of a person's career, most young professionals seek feedback to fix mistakes, learn how their company's systems work and improve productivity. Feedback from others can be valuable, but don't use it for approval or validation; instead, absorb all criticism as positive suggestions for improvement.

Then, after about five years, many mid-career professionals view feedback more defensively. They fear their boss will think they should 'know better' than to make mistakes with so many years of experience.

Finally, once you rise to a leadership position and have others reporting to you, listening to feedback takes on even greater importance and responsibility, because feedback is a vital tool that helps leaders spot problems and opportunities. So no matter what stage of your career you're in currently—new hire, mid-level manager, or top leader—avoid the temptation to ignore feedback. Instead, reflect on it. Decode it. And apply it in powerful ways.

Think of it like this—if you ate food and did not allow your body to digest it, you would feel bloated and sick. Similarly, when you receive feedback at work, you should take the time to reflect on it and absorb important lessons. While our body digests food automatically, active listening requires that we pause to LOL—Listen, Observe, Learn.

Lastly, I find that when most people impulsively react or interrupt, it's because they feel like they'll be left out if they don't rush into the conversation and say something. Another form of this is when people fear that if they don't say something first, another person will have the same thought and beat them to it. Reject the need to always be the first person to speak or interrupt others like I used to do. Truly listen and absorb what others are saying, show respect, and take time to formulate a smart and memorable response. Or none at all.

'Listening is an art. We tend to talk more, listen less,' says Harsh Goenka. 'I am reminded of a Buddhist monk who was quiet. People asked him, "Why are you quiet?" And he said, "Because I must have something to say that can improve upon the sound of silence." Most of us listen to answer, but we should listen to understand and sometimes to empathize.'

Two Powerful Listening Techniques

Let's learn two powerful listening techniques. They are simple to learn and fun to use. Better still, they will make you stand out from the crowd positively.

The first is called the 'summarizing takeaway' technique. Here's how it works. Imagine you're in a two-hour group meeting at work. The conversation is free-flowing and all over the place, with multiple ideas and solutions discussed. Toward the end of the meeting, you use the 'summarizing takeaway' technique like this: 'We covered a lot of important ground today. To make sure nothing falls through the cracks, I want to highlight seven key action items and takeaways we developed so we can hit the ground running.' You then go on to summarize the takeaway points or action items you absorbed through strong listening during the meeting.

The result: everyone in the room will think to themselves: *Wow. She's the reliable one in the room. She's always listening—even when we were going all over the place. I don't know where she came up with all those points, because I had forgotten a couple of them already. She adds value and keeps us organized and on- point.* Try it. It doesn't matter if you've only been with the company a couple of months. Speak up! People *always* respect a strong listener. You'll be amazed at the positive impact and reputation you'll create over time.

The second listening tool is the 'customized follow-up' technique. This is particularly useful during interviews, but it can be applied anytime someone wraps up a conversation by asking: 'Do you have any questions for me?' Imagine you're in an interview for a job as a coder. After thirty minutes of discussion between you and the interviewer, you are asked if you have any questions. Beginner job-seekers will usually come prepared with two or three generic questions based on information they found on the company's website or Wikipedia listing. That's a missed opportunity. Instead, you want to ask a customized question based on the interaction you *just had*. This tells the interviewer you pay attention. It also proves you think fast on your feet and remain focused and engaged. Use the 'customized follow-up'. It's a pro move.

Constructive vs Unprofessional Feedback

Now that you have some strong listening tools, it's important to know what kind of feedback to absorb versus the kind you should not listen to. When Vani Kola and I discuss her views on listening, she stresses that listening is a soft skill that we all must work on throughout our lifetimes—and that part of effective listening involves knowing what kind of feedback to accept versus what to ignore. 'Listening is one of those lifelong skills we need to continuously work on and improve. It's a fine balance,' says Kola. 'You have to know when to listen but also when not to listen.

Anecdotally, when I wanted to be an engineer because I loved math, and very few women were engineers, no one in my family approved, and my mother cried for days. But it was very important then to not listen to anyone and have self-conviction.' Vani's insight is hugely important. Listening doesn't equal obeying. Instead, it means taking in another person's feedback but then deciding your own course based on your values, goals and ambition. Moreover, there will also be times when people cross boundaries and say things you should push back against.

> *'Somehow, everything would always end with a simple "your parents really haven't taught you anything at all, have they?". I have been born and raised in a big city as a confident young woman, and yet I wouldn't know how to tackle that situation.'*
>
> —Kriti (31), digital marketing professional, Mumbai

There is no beating around the bush—what happened with Kriti is not okay. If someone aggressively attacks you on a purely personal level that is not based on the quality of your work, then that is unacceptable behaviour that is over the line and unprofessional. Full stop. Some people believe reporting such actions to human resources creates more problems than it solves. Only you can make that decision. But one thing you should do is stand up for yourself. How? Like this: 'I welcome you correcting my mistakes and helping me improve, but making fun of me personally is uncalled for and over the line. Let's please stay focused on the work.' Could the person continue using degrading language? Yes. But at least you have gone on record and established a clear bright line they should not cross.

Thankfully, most work-related feedback comes in a more appropriate form. When someone gives you constructive feedback—even if it reflects negatively on a mistake you made—thank them. Those two words—'thank you'—can melt a lot of negative reactions and make a positive impact. So don't ration your use of 'thank you'. People will remember you positively for using this phrase. In addition, showing gratitude lets colleagues know you are eager to learn from your errors. Your employer will respect your desire to improve. It also demonstrates that you are not insecure or defensive but are instead a lifelong learner, determined to grow. That's a win-win for you and your company.

Feedback Is a Two-Way Street

Imagine if you had a 'flag' on your desk or wore a hat that said 'I welcome feedback! I won't be defensive or sulk. I promise I take feedback well!' Now imagine how others would think about you over time. What would that do to your career now and in the future? The impact would be profound. Why? Because feedback is a two-way street. The more you listen to others, the more they will be willing to listen to you.

'I take the younger twenty-two- and twenty-three-year-olds to coffee; they're usually eager to talk so they'll say everything out loud, then I patiently point out where they went wrong and how they could have done better. A mentor did this for me, so now I try to do it for others.'

—Pranav (34), assistant manager, Gurgaon

Pranav's approach is one designed for success. I say this because developing friendships and mentors inside your company is important. Seeking help from colleagues with more experience is a good way to learn. Remember: feedback doesn't always have to be from superiors to juniors—it can be from peer to peer as well. You can gain helpful knowledge from peers who have been with the company even just a few months longer than you.

Also, if you've been at the receiving end of unprofessional feedback, break the cycle by treating others with respect. Build people up through constructive feedback. They will never forget the professional courtesy.

One way you can implement this is similar to the way OYO's Ritesh Agarwal does. 'I take feedback very seriously and spend a lot of time with it. One feedback I remember well was that at group meetings I would speak a lot and I would think everyone else was speaking a lot more. The feedback in a lot of conversations was that I would cut people off from speaking, and not enable them to speak their minds or create impact. Now I've moved from being the leader in a conversation to being the moderator,' says Agarwal.

Ritesh understands that truly listening to feedback means being willing to act on it and improve. If he can find the time to do that, so can you and I. After all, great listeners make great leaders. It is a soft skill worth investing time and energy in to succeed.

5 Core Takeaways

- Eliminate distractions. Be mentally 'present' when others are communicating. Avoid 'switching off' when you're done speaking.

- Eating without digesting leaves a person bloated and sick. Likewise, after listening, you must take the time to 'digest', absorb, reflect and apply the feedback you've been given.
- Using the 'summarizing takeaway' technique during meetings will establish you as a reliable and organized listener. When someone asks if you have any questions, use the 'customized follow-up' technique based on the conversation you just had—not a generic question you prepared in advance.
- Know the difference between constructive feedback versus overly personal and unprofessional attacks. Accept and appreciate good-quality feedback—even if it is bluntly stated or highlights your errors. But if people clearly cross a professional line through personal attacks, stand up for yourself.
- Feedback is a two-way street. And it doesn't always have to be top down from superiors to juniors. Look for opportunities to receive and share quality feedback with peers to build professional friendships and growth.

Call to Action

1. This chapter is to tell you to be **selfish**. You must stop trying to go through life focusing only on what you want others to think of you. Working or living to 'impress' others is a waste of time and reaps no results. People will form their own views anyway. So be selfish. Live by your own goals and benchmarks. The day you do that, I assure you, you will listen, you will observe, you will learn.

2. Remember: To practice LOL, you need to keep your mouth shut but your eyes and ears open. Your mind has to be silent and attentive, otherwise you're going to be listening only to yourself (your view on what you heard) day in and day out, without letting fresh thoughts and ideas enter. How far can you go with that?

6

Empathy Is a Sign of Strength, Not Weakness

Sometimes, when you're battling difficulties or feeling low, you just need somebody to relate to the way you're feeling at that moment. That's called empathy—understanding how someone else is feeling. It's a powerful tool to bond at all levels, and it's always a two-way street. Give empathy, and you will receive it too. It can get you through many tough days.

Things were certainly tough many years ago, when the media company I had co-founded was on the verge of collapse and bankruptcy. Things were miserable; it felt like the walls were closing in. I gave a talk to about 130 employees. It was bad news, but it needed to be conveyed, and in such a way that people were left feeling hopeful and inspired. Deep down, I believed we would figure out a way to climb out of the hole we were in, but the pressure weighed on my chest like a stone.

Shortly after I finished speaking to everyone, one of my junior colleagues, Derek, approached me. 'Hey, Ronnie, tomorrow evening if you're free, please come to my home for dinner,' he said.

'I appreciate the invite, but I'm really not up to it,' I told him. 'I've just got so much on my mind that I don't think I'd be a fun dinner guest.'

He didn't take no for an answer. He said, 'Of course you have a lot on your mind, but it would be good for you to break up your routine and clear your mind for an hour or two.' So, I agreed to go. Derek took me to his home where he introduced me to his brother, who happened to be a fascinating individual. He began sharing his life's story, about the huge obstacles he had overcome in his personal life. As I sat and listened to the challenges and tragedies he overcame, I started thinking, *How can I feel the way I do about my situation? There are so many people out there in the world with far bigger and more complex problems than mine!*

After dinner, I told Derek, 'Wow. I can't thank you enough for tonight.' On my way home, I realized what his plan had been all along: to give me a fresh perspective by allowing me to relate and empathize with someone else's difficulties.

Empathy vs Sympathy

The soft skill of empathy can transform a company's culture. That's particularly true when those in management encourage it and practise it themselves. But you have to understand what the word empathy means and what it doesn't.

When most people hear the world 'empathy', they immediately think it's the same thing as 'sympathy'. Even though the two words rhyme, they have very different meanings.

> *'I've always wondered how to be empathetic towards my seniors. We expect empathy but it feels like if my behaviour was empathetic in return, would I come across as someone who is sucking up to the seniors?'*
>
> —Naresh (24), PR professional, Jaipur

Naresh, it does not matter where you are in your career, whether you're just beginning or have risen to the management level, you will benefit from showing your colleagues empathy. Kiran Mazumdar-Shaw of Biocon tells me she believes empathy fuels inspiration and builds trust. That's absolutely true in my experience. Also, others are likely to return the favour by showing you empathy and understanding when you need it most. So that's a win-win. The key, of course, is learning the right time and way to express empathy at work.

Empathy Isn't about Being Soft or Weak

One of the concerns many people have about workplace empathy is that they will be seen as pushovers, soft and weak. This is a concern particularly for team leaders and managers. Aditi describes her situation and dilemma.

> *'I do try to empathize when someone is experiencing a tough situation, but I don't want anyone to take undue advantage and let their performance suffer. I need to ensure team performance never suffers and that requires some sternness.'*
>
> —Aditi (33), team leader, Bangalore

To Aditi and all other managers, let's be clear: showing empathy does not mean letting people walk all over you. Not at all. A manager can be strong and maintain high expectations while still showing empathy to their employees and peers when it's appropriate. It's about recognizing that we're all human beings who have a life outside of work that occasionally brings its own challenges and difficulties. So how can you show empathy without appearing soft or easily manipulated?

Let's say you're the leader of a fifteen-person sales team. You have a daily 9 a.m. Zoom meeting where everyone logs on. You brief the team for the first fifteen minutes, and then everyone gets to work presenting their ideas and updates. For the last couple of days, you've noticed that Sita is not logging on until 9.14 a.m. You pull her aside and say, 'Sita, what is the problem? You seem to be closing your deals, but are you being stubborn and thinking the first fifteen minutes of the meeting are not relevant for you? What is the problem?' She replies, 'No, I'm having a network problem.' You then show empathy, but also call out the BS answer by responding like this: 'Well, I'm happy to first talk with you about anything that's going on in your life. If there's a personal situation affecting your networking, then I'm happy to listen. But something isn't adding up for me. Why are you having a network problem exactly between 9 a.m. and 9.14 a.m., and not from 9.15 onwards?'

Such a response leaves room for empathy for any real personal situation Sita may genuinely be experiencing in her life, while also highlighting how her explanation doesn't make much sense. The goal is to give someone enough space to share a legitimate problem but not so much that they will attempt to manipulate you with a sob story.

A Little Goes a Long Way

You can be both strong and empathetic at the same time. But you may wonder how often you should demonstrate empathy at work. After all, we go to work in order to solve problems, serve customers and create value—not constantly talk about our own personal problems and emotions. So how often is too often when it comes to empathy?

My answer is that a little bit goes a long way. If you're constantly being 'fake nice' and approaching every situation from the perspective of personal emotion and feelings, people will start to think you're insincere. Most situations at work are about solving technical problems, hitting deadlines, strategy and execution—issues that have very little to do with relating to a person's feelings. So it's not as though one must go around the office offering everyone hugs and therapy.

> *'If a relative of mine falls ill, I'll be asked if I really need the time off. It's such an awkward spot to be placed in, because if I didn't need some days off why would I ask?'*
> —Manjot (27), banking sector employee, Ludhiana

To not be empathetic or in a situation like Manjot's is not okay. When a colleague experiences serious hardships or personal challenges, it's important to offer genuine empathy. The best way to show empathy is through focused listening with the goal of understanding and relating to the other person's problem. That's it. Don't feel like you have to 'solve' their problem or be a therapist. Just take time to lend them an ear and your heart will do the rest. Another bonus: being in service to another person brings one joy. 'Taking the time to be empathetic will create not just a deeper relationship, but also create more joy for you,' says Vani Kola. A little empathy really goes a long way.

Leadership and Empathy Go Hand in Hand

A wise person once said, 'People don't care what you know until they know that you care.' There's a lot of truth in that. Leadership has many dimensions, but one of them is letting people know you care about what happens to them. If empathy is at the back of your mind, you will relate and connect to people better. You will also come across as more inspiring. The sooner in your career you develop empathy, the better, says Harsh Goenka. 'Doing good for others is extremely important, and it's not something you do at 45–50. Having empathy and doing good is something you need to do from early on.'

If you're a team leader, manager or even a CEO, you may be a very tough and demanding boss, but your employees could still say to themselves, 'I'm being driven and led well by someone who pushes me hard but still cares. He really gets and understands me.' When an employee feels that way, there's no limit to how hard they will work to give the team their best and brightest work. Suneeta Reddy of Apollo Hospitals tells me that her experience of being pushed propelled her to be the corporate leader she is today. 'People are a little bit tougher on women,' says Reddy. 'My first year at work, the CFO told me you're here because you're the boss's daughter. Don't look for empathy all the time. I went back—I went to ICMR, I did a tough course on finance, I studied treasury management. So I am glad they were aggressive, and tough with me. When you don't expect empathy, you do much better.'

As Suneeta's experience shows, leaders sometimes show tough love, that is its own form of empathy, to propel one forward.

Finally, remember that when it comes to empathy, it doesn't have to only be expressed in tough times. You can relate to others and show understanding in good times, too. The birth of a child or grandchild, marriage, a promotion, overcoming a major health challenge—there are many occasions when you can empathize with others. Leaders gain respect when they relate to people during both their high moments and low moments. Look for opportunities to do both.

Peer-to-Peer Empathy Builds Unity

It's easy to think about empathy as something that only applies to how leaders interact with employees. Not true. In fact, one of the most powerful and impactful displays of empathy can be seen when peers at all levels of an organization begin showing empathy for each other. I was moved by Amitabh Kant's testimony about how his colleagues supported him during his darkest hours. 'I have been through such terrible things in my own career. At one stage, I had run afoul of the government in Kerala and I was victimized. I was without a job for almost ten months, and I got a lot of empathy from many of my colleagues. But that's what made me see through those very dark days when I thought that's the end of my career.' As Kant's experience demonstrates, bonds of trust, respect and unity form when you know that the people you work alongside genuinely care and relate to you on a deeper level.

Now, maybe you're thinking to yourself, 'Well, my company's culture is different. It's cut-throat and too competitive for all this empathy stuff.' Let's be clear: if you work in a company with a culture that's not known for being empathetic, you can stand out from the crowd positively by setting a new tone and direction. By slowly showing your peers empathy over time, you will gain their respect, trust and loyalty. That's good for them and good for you, because it builds bonds that strengthen team unity. The key is starting as soon as possible, says HUL's Sanjeev Mehta. 'Many times you will hear youngsters say, "I don't like the style of my boss; when I become like him I'll do it differently." And to them I say, "Don't wait to become the boss but develop those traits today itself." The same is true for empathy. Empathy is not for someone weaker than you, it's for someone different from you.'

Give it a try. Show a little empathy to your peers, then watch it spread.

5 Core Takeaways

- 'Empathy' and 'sympathy' are not the same thing. Empathy is being able to relate to how someone is feeling, even if you don't share the same emotion. Sympathy is feeling exactly what someone else is feeling.
- You can be strong and empathetic at the same time. Empathy isn't about being soft, weak or just a shoulder to cry on. Not at all. It's about showing your humanity while still maintaining your authority.
- Being 'fake nice' all the time isn't empathy. Save expressions of empathy for situations that truly call for it. A little bit goes a long way.
- Leaders know the power of empathy. People work harder and respect leaders who genuinely care about them. Companies with an empathetic culture are more likely to thrive.
- Empathy isn't just for leaders. Peer-to-peer empathy builds strong bonds of team unity.

Call to Action

1. When someone asks me what's one of my biggest strengths, I tell them that while I don't suffer

mediocrity and tend to switch off with someone who is full of excuses and defensive answers, I have learnt to forgive and move on. Forgiving does not mean just accepting, but also moving forward. I've realized that you need to be secure, confident and strong in order to forgive. Only insecure and weak people cannot forgive.

2. I can say I've done over 2000 exit interviews of team members, met hundreds of managers, leaders and even entrepreneurs who have had setbacks, and the one common factor I took away from the ones who could not make it, could not stick it out or faced temporary failure, was that they made the maximum excuses—it was never 'their fault'. This one trait is the difference between losers and followers vs winners and leaders.

7

Future-Proof Your Career

Throughout my career, two questions have followed me more than any others. First, 'What's your biggest learning?' And second, 'What's your biggest failure?' My answer to both is the same: my biggest learning and failure are yet to happen. I mean it. That's got to be the North Star in your thinking throughout your career—that your biggest teachable moment and biggest failure are still to come. When you think like that, it opens your mind up to pursuing a life of learning and upgrading one's skills, because it reminds you that you've still got so much to learn.

That's been my experience. When I started my career, certain things like innovation, creativity and marketing came naturally to me, but I lacked deep commercial acumen and an understanding of numbers and financials, and knowledge of technology. So, I made it a goal to take two or three years to fill in the gaps. Taking that time to go deep in my knowledge through structured learning made all the difference.

Why? Because every once in a while, you may have an 'a-ha' moment and learn a new trick or tip, but you need to really invest the time to go deep and experience ongoing learning to build a superior depth of understanding and expertise that outlasts casual insights.

Upgrading your skills to stay relevant by learning the best and newest techniques and tools is vital for being a lifelong learner. This could mean different things for each of us. You may want to stay within the domain or sector you are in, and so may want to learn more and specialize—or maybe you want to change career paths and learn a new vocation. Or you simply want to be more rounded and feel that while you understand marketing or technology, you need to get smart on leadership or finance. And remember, you are going to face multiple crossroads in your career when you feel the need to learn more. It's not going to happen just once. Lifelong learning is an essential part of the modern professional world. Professionals must continuously upgrade their knowledge throughout their careers. 'The days of being guided by company or boss are long gone,' says C.P. Gurnani. 'So if you're waiting for them to chart a course for you, then you have bigger things to be worried about.'

If you want to 'future-proof' your career—that is, guard it and protect it against unknown events—you have to be a lifelong learner. There's no other choice. First comes the realization that you may not be at your best at your job, that things have changed, that different talent has come into the company, and you feel you need to know more, learn more. Once you have realized this need, don't think too much or wait for a crisis to hit you or formal feedback from your company to 'up your game'. The world is your oyster.

Failure to Upgrade Skills Costs Far More in the End

Before we talk about the benefits and methods of lifelong learning and revamping one's knowledge, I want to address one of the biggest reasons working professionals fail to learn on an ongoing basis. Some people think to themselves, *Look, I already went to school. I got my college degree(s). It cost a lot of money. Plus, I hated studying all the time. So, this new wave of learning online, carrying on with my job while having access to the best courses, faculty, industry professionals and universities in the world doesn't seem like it's worth the financial cost. Dividing my already limited money and time feels unnecessary*. That line of thinking, while understandable, completely misses the reality of what's happening right now in the global workforce. Redundancy will be high, and the need for specialization, being sharper, more knowledgeable and updated in your job, and learning all the soft skills needed to up your game are here to stay.

> *'No one is irreplaceable in our sector; people are as good as street-side shopping—you'll find hundred others if one doesn't match your bargain offer. The minute a new, younger person can do it better, you're at risk.'*
>
> —Deepika (34), operations lead, Pune

Is Deepika's fear realistic or is she just being paranoid? If you ask me, between technological advancements and consumer changes, whether we like it or not, a massive shift occurs every four or five years in the methods and technological tools companies use to do business. (Just think about how much faster and better the software and technological tools you use now are compared to even a few years ago.) There's no use kidding ourselves; employees can't stand still any more. While our parents and grandparents may have been able to stick in the same job for decades with no additional training, we cannot. The days of a slow-and-steady chronological career climb have been replaced by a fast-changing world that demands constant and concurrent updating of one's skills and knowledge. Ritesh Agarwal says the key to lifelong learning is to get in the habit as soon as one can. 'Lifelong learning is something everyone wants to do but they often procrastinate about it,' Agarwal explains. 'Unless the situation gets bad, people often don't invest in it. In the early stage of your career, it's important to forward-invest in all other abilities, and not just in doing your job.' As I said earlier, lifelong learning is a necessity because the ground is constantly shifting under our feet.

Ritesh is right that the sooner in your career you become a lifelong learner the better. But no matter what stage of your career you're in, you're going to realize why lifelong learning is the best way to future-proof your career. For example, if you're in the beginning of your career, a couple of years into your job it might hit you that maybe you started working too early and without some core knowledge and experience. Then, by the time you're thirty to thirty-five years old, the super confidence of the first few years shifts to more of a 'stability' mindset, which makes you less willing to take risks. Without lifelong learning to upgrade your knowledge and further specialize your skills, insecurity can creep in.

As for mid-career professionals between the ages of forty and fifty-five, you begin to feel like you have 'arrived' and deserve respect for your years of service and experience. Then you're confronted with the harsh reality: each year, a new generation of employees enters the workforce with greater analytical knowledge of future software, data and systems, and an understanding of the speed of modern corporate competitiveness.

Vijay Shekhar Sharma says it's all about maintaining relevance for the future. 'When we overestimate what we have achieved and live in the past, we do not learn and we do not try to be relevant for the future,' says Sharma. He believes this so deeply, in fact, that he doesn't even call himself Paytm's chief executive officer but instead says he is the 'chief relevance officer'. The reason Vijay does this is to maintain focus on always making sure he and his company are future-proofing to remain relevant. So how can you and I do the same? What's the solution?

This is *not about* endlessly adding degree after degree; rather, the solution is adding skill after skill through an ongoing cycle of lifelong learning to upgrade your knowledge and specialize in your area of expertise. Specialization is a huge part of lifelong learning and all roads lead to it. We had Gen X, Gen Y and Gen Z, but now we have Gen S—Generation Specialization. The days of being a generalist are numbered. We saw and continue to see that during the COVID-19 pandemic, where more generalists were cut out and specialists kept on. A critical part of lifelong learning is pausing to examine one's career path to chart the next five years. If your goal is to move up the earnings ladder, being a specialist is mandatory. If you're in an area that most consider a generalist position, such as sales, your goal must be to turn your sales skills into specialized knowledge. That might mean engaging in deep learning about one or two core sectors, learning product and service, and acquiring digital skills to reach and sell to newer and larger demographics. Bottom line: specialization through lifelong learning keeps you relevant and growing.

And if all that doesn't convince you, maybe this will: the cost of losing one's

job or promotion is much greater than the time and resources a person would invest in keeping their skills fresh and current. So now that we see the necessity of constantly growing and specializing our skills throughout our career, let's explore the benefits.

Identifying 'Trucks' and Trends

> *'The growth prospects in my sector and what lies next is a point I get worried about often. How do I predict what the next buzz will be, and how do I ensure my skillset can get me there?'*
>
> —Akram (26), IT sector profession, Hyderabad

Akram's concern is a legitimate one; how can you know what the next wave of upgraded skills are if you can't see ahead beyond a year or more and constantly be aware of new trends, changing consumer desires and spends and the disruptive technology that will enable all of it? The answer, of course, is that you learn first-hand from experts who know the emerging trends and dangers in your industry. That's why lifelong learning is the heartbeat of career success. To everyone who shares the same worry as Akram, I would say one of the keys to professional success is learning how to identify the 'trucks' (dangers) speeding toward your industry. You also want to learn how to spot the 'trends' (opportunities) that can take you and your company to the next level. And again, that's why revamping your skills with the help of expert instructors is critical, because these people already *know* what trucks and trends to look out for! Being well prepared for all eventualities, yet not letting that slow down your growth, is key. The more time you spend to understand what crisis can come and hit you, while you simultaneously look for trends that will propel your growth and make you stand out, the more well prepared you are.

While there are no 100 per cent guarantees to know what lies around the corner, learning the newest methods, techniques and technologies in your industry will keep you on the cutting edge of innovation. The only way to know what's coming is to pay attention and stay plugged in to what's going on. And the only way to do that is to constantly gain new knowledge and skills. Once you make this your mindset, exciting opportunities begin to open up. For example, in my career I've moved sectors several times, from media to rural and social work to sports to education. Deep learning trains your brain to know what to look for when you enter a new and complex market or sector. It's all about keeping your mind sharp through constant learning and upgrading skills and knowledge.

Consider this: by the time a person completes a college degree, many of the software applications and technological platforms they learnt as a first-year student are already old, or obsolete by the time they graduate. Now if that's true while one is in college, it is equally true in the professional world. So what exactly does lifelong learning look like in practical terms?

Aim for Deep Learning

We've seen the necessity of gaining new skills throughout our career, as well as how upgrading our knowledge can help us spot the trucks and trends coming our way. So what should we actually *do*? Also, what's the best process for busy professionals with a job?

Let's say you are a digital marketer who specializes in social media. Simply reading books or watching YouTube videos about your area of expertise is not enough. For one, given how fast social media moves, by the time a book is published, much will already have changed. (Even as I am writing this, Instagram launched Reels to compete with TikTok.) But beyond the speed of technological growth, there is a profound difference in reading about how something works and rolling up your sleeves and learning how to do it yourself.

So how does one do that, especially if you already work full time or have a busy family life? Answer: online training with experts who allow you to build 'deep knowledge'—learnings that stick because they came through hands-on experience. At upGrad, the company I co-founded for both soft and hard skills—a lifelong partner to everyone from college-going kids to fifty-five-year-olds—we knew it wouldn't be enough simply to hire a world-class faculty of experts. So we spent years developing and perfecting a curriculum and online learning environment that creates deep knowledge through hands-on interactive experiences. Then, we gave students one-on-one time directly with their expert instructors to go even deeper. It's a big part of the reason we are so highly rated by students and the companies that hire them. This method is far superior to, say, just taking a short two- or three-month refresher course that scrapes the surface but doesn't reach the depth of learning.

Growth Can Happen Horizontally, Too

Beyond building deep knowledge through online training, you can also learn and grow by sharpening skills in your current job position. Again, recall the example of the digital marketer who specializes in social media. If her core responsibilities involve buying and placing social media adverts on Instagram and Facebook, perhaps she will expand her skills by learning the tools and tactics for Twitter or YouTube advertising as well. While her job still involves Instagram and Facebook advertising, she's learning horizontally by acquiring additional social media advertising skills and strategies that will make her more valuable to her employer.

> *'Newbies always want to grow vertically; no one wants to grow horizontally. We shift jobs vertically but we aren't trained enough to handle it. Especially when we grow vertically before acing our current job role, because then we get busy getting work done by our juniors and forgetting how to do our own job.'*
>
> —Rahil (29), assistant sales manager, Hyderabad

Reread Rahil's experience, remember it and learn from it. Step back and think from your company's perspective. If Employee A knows how to perform three core skills but Employee B knows how to perform six, assuming they are equally talented at their job, Employee B adds twice the value simply because they took the time to develop twice as many skills.

So, look for horizontal opportunities to learn inside your current position.

Often, all it takes is being willing to learn something new. Give it a shot.

Consider Switching Things Up

After a few years in your job, it is not uncommon to begin to feel 'stuck' or to fall into a 'slump' phase. Sometimes, people get bored because they don't see the value their work adds for their company. Other times, it's because they get so used to doing the same thing over and over that their work feels robotic.

> *'What if I become just another brick in the wall? I wanted to do a lot when I was twenty-one, but eight years in, I can't help feeling like my work makes no actual difference, not even to my company, forget the world.'*
>
> —Ankit (29), marketing consultant, Delhi

What Ankit is experiencing is a common feeling we can all identify with. If this happens, don't panic. But do recognize that this mindset will make it harder for you to find the motivation to continue learning and growing until you take steps to fix it. One way to break the monotony is to switch departments or divisions. This is not easy as most lateral shifts mean you are reinterviewing for a new role. Maybe it's the right time to do a top-up course. Depending on a company's size and structure, this is not always possible. But if it is, a new department can allow you to explore a different domain with new team dynamics to mix things up. Best of all, being around new talent can lead to the organic upgrading of one's skills while on the job. Another option is asking your boss if you can work on a passion project—a work initiative that you can tackle that will force you to learn new skills. Even if your boss says no, your request will likely be seen as further evidence of your desire to add value and grow professionally. Win-win. But for all this, there needs to be a strong intent and sense of urgency.

5 Core Takeaways

- It costs far more *not* to keep your skills current and up to date than it does to invest the time and resources in upgrading one's knowledge.
- Lifelong learning is one of the best ways to spot trucks (dangers) and trends (opportunities).
- The best type of lifelong learning involves gaining deep knowledge through practical, hands-on training with expert guidance and instruction.
- Professional growth isn't always vertical; you can improve your skills horizontally as well by learning new techniques and skills within your current position.
- Switching departments or developing a passion project at work can give you wide exposure to new knowledge.

Call to Action

1. 'Today' is a much more effective and powerful word for you than 'tomorrow'. Putting off things for tomorrow has never made a great manager or leader. That does not mean everything has to be done today. Preplanning is critical, but in your planning and in your actions think 'today'. The world and consumers are changing too fast and so you have to ensure that your 'tomorrow' does not lead you to yesterday and irrelevance.
2. How badly do you want something? If you want something badly enough, you're going to give it your all. Always have two (not more) things you want

badly in life—really badly—and it will bring such focus, such hard work and such sacrifice that you never knew existed inside you. This is the secret sauce to success today and most days. Start this now. Do not just 'TRY' this and stop but do it for the rest of your life. Also, your age is never a factor for career success—it's always how badly you want it.

8

The Multitasking Myth

My dog taught me that multitasking is overrated and often counterproductive.

Yes, you read that correctly, my dog. Here's what happened.

In the first seven years of my working life I took great pride in being a multitasker. I even gave myself a nickname, 'MT', for multitasker. Back then, multitasking was my addiction; it gave me a 'high' thinking about how super-efficient, productive and ahead of the game I was. It got so bad, in fact, that it spilled over into my personal life and made me antisocial, even with my own family. My wife, Zarina, and my daughter, Trishya, and I would go to a restaurant for dinner, but instead of chatting and enjoying a leisurely meal together, I would stare into my plate and shovel food into my mouth quickly, with my brain a million kilometres away.

During this time, I ignored the early signs that my multitasking addiction was out of control. I felt exhausted, had no energy, and was socially distant from friends and family. Had I taken an honest assessment, I would have realized that I was clearly less productive, unfocused, all over the place mentally, and distracted. I got less things done that were high quality. Another early sign: I gained 4 kg because I was so busy multitasking during meals that I ate more and focused less on what I was eating!

Then two things happened that woke me up and helped me break my absurd multitasking addiction. The first of these moments was in a super important meeting for which I had prepared well, and I delivered a strong performance when it was my turn to talk. But then, in my multitasking arrogance, I switched off for ten minutes to catch up on my messages. After all, I was superhuman and could switch off and on anytime, right? Wrong! As it turned out, those ten minutes were the most important part of the entire meeting. When my attention returned to the room, I made an utter fool of myself by asking questions everyone had already answered and bringing up topics they had just discussed. They stared at me like I was an idiot. I embarrassed myself in front of the people I wanted to impress and made a sour impression.

But the final straw that helped me break my multitasking addiction came when I took my dog for a walk. There I was with my earphones on, making calls, recording notes, trying to do several things at once, and I didn't see my golden Labrador playfully lunge at me with the Frisbee I had thrown him. I was so distracted that I fell backwards, stretched out my hand to break my fall, and fractured my wrist. That was it! The message to me was loud and clear: I had to change my ways, fast. I did. And I've never looked back. It's been a total game-changer for me. Today I get *so* much more done because I do *NOT get multidistracted in my pursuit to* multitask!

The Multitasking Myth

Let me break up multitasking into three categories.

1. Multitasking when you are permanently in a state of distraction: This is the worst. You want to do four things at the same time, and can't focus on anything at hand because your eye is on the next message in your inbox, your ear just heard the phone ring, your mind is on three things you don't want to forget. Yet, you are in the middle of this important conversation or meeting, where if you miss out on the important takeaways, you are not going to be able to complete the assignment later.
2. Multitasking when you are overwhelmed: You are constantly trying to catch your tail and finish your tasks. Remember, half the time, you are overwhelmed with the exhaustion of feeling like there is so much to do—you have so many tasks but not enough hours in the day. Well, the simple point here is that multitasking is not allowing you to stop, prioritize and plan. It's a vicious circle. You feel that if you pause to take time to think, plan and prioritize, you may become even more behind on your work. So you just keep going until . . . well, until nothing—as it's not going to change till your mindset changes and you realize that the fault, at most times, is not on the tasks, the company, your boss or peers, but your inability to prioritize, plan and in some cases say 'no'.

3. Setting multiple goals for yourself: No one says you need to go through life just doing one thing at a time. So you've set out to launch three new products this month, revamp your tech team, and a lot more. Well, go ahead, plan and set your multitasking goals. Multitasking without the addiction of distraction and being overwhelmed is productive multitasking. Every day, I am multitasking and getting things done. but I have learned the importance of doing that one thing in the moment, which means I get a lot done in the day. When I am in a meeting, I am 100 per cent in that meeting and am also trying to ensure everyone else is mentally present as well. When I am having a discussion with five reverse-migrated farmers who have gone back to their villages, I can easily think of replying to three WhatsApp messages while they get to the point. But then I will lose out on the crux of the conversation. If I'm in a brainstorming session for a product launch's marketing campaign, my best ideas come by just listening to everything and being there rather than just saying my bit and then switching off while others talk. When I was writing this book, there were late nights or early mornings with lots of distractions, and lots more to get done in the day, but then I realized there's no point in writing a book if you don't give it your everything. The discipline of not being permanently distracted has allowed me to get a lot done in a day. If I put in one hour of my time to mindfully prepare and review for a particular task allows me to be at my best and not feel overwhelmed.

Let's be honest—we have all bought into the myth that multitasking is a positive thing with few, if any, downsides. It seems logical, right? Who doesn't want to get 'more' done and cram as much as possible into each day? The belief that multitasking is always a good thing is so universally believed that we never even question it. But we should. Multitasking has several negatives. 'Multitasking often becomes the enemy of excellence,' says Ritesh Agarwal. 'It shouldn't come at the cost of excellence.'

So let's look at some terrible reasons why people multitask. The biggest one is multitasking to impress others. It's normal to feel the temptation to always seem 'busy' so that others view you as productive. But that's putting on an act, not executing your work effectively. Multitasking to show off for your boss or co-worker never ends well.

> *'A friend of mine tried to kick off a start-up, and thought that once it picks up he will leave his current job. He was barely sleeping, his quality of work was declining, and our boss noticed it too.'*
>
> —Shivam (31), technology expert, Pune

We should learn from what Shivam's friend experienced. A key sign that a person has fallen for the multitasking myth is when they justify mediocre quality by being 'just too busy' or having 'too much to do and not enough time to do it'. The solution for low-quality work is never to add more tasks into your day. In fact, it's the opposite. If you find yourself underperforming or overwhelmed, shift your focus to the big and important objectives.

As the old saying goes, less really is more. And, of course, when multitasking gets in the way of your relationships with others, that's another sign it's time to reassess. C.P. Gurnani says he tries to avoid multitasking when spending time with others because 'giving someone your undivided attention is the biggest respect you can give them'. Wise words we should all follow.

Focus More on Goals, Less on Tasks

I already shared earlier that multitasking has different aspects. It's very important for us to be aware when we are multitasking. My first alert is when I am distracted or not fully concentrating on what I'm doing at that moment. I could be talking to someone while looking at my devices or being elsewhere mentally while attending a meeting—my mind is whirring with five other tasks I am dying to do at that very minute. Well, STOP—you are not going to get anything done properly, and you are going to feel stressed and wonder why the days seem so long while being unproductive. If you are constantly distracted, you are in a multitasking danger zone!

> *'In an MBA, we are constantly in classes, quizzes, projects, internships, etc. Maybe it's all in preparation for actual work life?'*
>
> —Tarana (25), HR professional, Chandigarh

Let me take on Tarana's question. Look closely at the word 'multitasking'.

Break it down. 'Multi' means many. A 'task' means a smaller job. So, when we talk about multitasking we're really talking about the many small steps or jobs that are a means to a much bigger objective. And what is that much bigger objective called? A GOAL. Now, imagine if you had to do 'multi-goaling' every day and stuff several major goals into a work day. It wouldn't work. Even saying the word—'multi-goaling'—sounds silly, because it is. A goal is big. Important. An objective that requires concentration and focus.

Learn to stop and ask yourself: what is a task versus a goal? Remember: achieving goals *is* the goal! So don't get distracted with smaller, meaningless tasks that get in the way. Goals will get you results. Tasks will get you through a workday but not much more.

Employers judge professionals on the basis of whether they hit their targets and accomplish big goals, not on whether they can complete a list of smaller and less important tasks. That's another reason you should never multitask to impress others. You can multitask your whole career, but it will all be worth a big zero if your performance doesn't produce results. What's really impressive is a focused employee who doesn't allow 'busy work' to distract them from achieving big goals. That's the way to stand out in a crowd.

Maximum Productivity Requires Deep Focus

Now that we know multitasking leads to distraction, and that achieving goals should be our primary focus, you may be wondering how one can maximize productivity. One of the questions I get asked frequently is how I manage to be deeply active in so many diverse areas—such as having a deep commitment to EdTech with upGrad, doing social work with the Swades Foundation, carrying out high-impact storytelling with movies through RSVP, and yet still having time to author a book and mentor entrepreneurs, not to mention inspiring and cheering our U Mumba kabaddi team. People expect me to say that I multitask round the clock.

Not so. In fact, my method for being productive and achieving results has very little to do with multitasking.

It takes massive discipline.

Both require intense focus. If I try to multitask by answering emails, scanning videos and replying to WhatsApp messages during my deep preparation and goal planning, the results will be disastrous. One eye going to your left, the other eye going to your right—that's not multitasking. That's being cock-eyed. You're not a magician—you cannot be in multiple places at multiple times and expect to achieve top productivity. Do I get distracted at times during the day? Yes. Do I get tempted to multitask when I should be laser-focused instead? Sure. But what keeps me sane and making progress is discipline, planning for all possibilities, and setting short- and long-term goals. Let me expand. Firstly, even if I have a fourteen-hour workday, I make sure I stretch it for another thirty minutes—this is the most important use of thirty minutes of my time where I review the day and plan ahead. Without that, I am going to be unproductive the next day, and even the next month. That catch-up time allows me to be more prepared than all my peers for any and all tasks the next day. Secondly, goals for me are not just about new things, but things I would like to see change. At least half of my short-term goal setting is about what I want to do differently. Long-term goals keep me sane—they go far beyond the daily grind and will have more of a lasting impact. Put simply, one has to know when to multitask and when not to in order to maximize productivity.

Develop an Effective Morning Multitasking Routine

So far, we've discussed the downsides of multitasking and when not to do it. Now it's time to explore the beneficial aspects of multitasking.

To me, the time when multitasking is most beneficial and useful is during my daily morning walk. My legs and body burn calories. My mind gets clear about the day ahead (and probably burns more calories than my body does!). I voice-record my messages. I organize my agenda for the day. I soak in the sights and sounds around me. That sparks creative thoughts. That's productive multitasking—doing many things at once. Now, sometimes I take walks simply for relaxation and fresh air. Those are important too. When you need to 'switch off' for a bit, do so. And for goodness sake, do not strain your neck looking down at your phone. If the goal is to relax, then relax!

That's my morning multitasking routine. But you do what works best for you. Multitasking is best for doing easy tasks where mistakes are low-risk and unlikely. What's not a good idea is doing things like trying to craft your high-stakes sales presentation while bumping along on public transport. There are too many distractions then.

> *'I am always listening to music on my metro ride, but my friend finishes a part of her work in the metro. It's too crowded to even think, but she just seems to do it.*
>
> —Ambika (24), social media manager

I agree with Ambika. For something like that, you need to have undivided attention and focus so you can remember all your key points. Bottom line: effective multitasking is all about knowing when it's okay and beneficial to combine tasks versus when laser focus is required.

Take a Multitasking Break

Be honest: how many times while reading or listening to this book have you stopped to check your Instagram, WhatsApp, Twitter, Snapchat, Facebook or email? If you're like most people, the answer is several times. That's understandable. Tech distractions are everywhere, and we justify them as simply another form of 'multi tasking'.

But what if, for a day or two, you took a break from multitasking and instead used that time a different way? What if, instead of Zooming, Skyping, WhatsApping and rushing in and out of offices all the time, you focused on coming up with the best tech idea, product solution, marketing strategy or sales pitch? Now, perhaps you are worried about how it might look if your boss or team members were seen multitasking during that time and you weren't. But think about what would happen during the next meeting or Zoom session—while everyone is distracted and pretending to be paying attention, and you introduce your brilliant idea, plan or strategy, ask yourself: who will be remembered more? Those who 'looked busy'? Or you—the person who helped the company achieve a breakthrough? The answer is obvious. Try it. Take a break from multitasking and use that time to come up with the next big solution. You will be glad you did.

5 Core Takeaways

- The idea that there are no potential downsides to multitasking is wrong.
  When done incorrectly or out of a desire to impress others, multitasking can lead to distractions and mistakes.
- Focus on achieving a few big goals versus checking dozens of tasks off your to-do list.
- Maximum productivity is achieved through deep preparation, planning and discipline—not constant multitasking interruptions.
- Develop your own morning multitasking planning routine. Combine tasks where mistakes are unlikely or less important.
- Take a multitasking break. Use the extra time to focus on coming up with the next big idea or solution for your company. Your employer cares more about results than 'looking busy'.

Call to Action

1. Ask yourself: do you really enjoy multitasking? Let me ask you, when you sit with your mom or nani, what's

the one thing you enjoy most from your interaction with either of them? Why is it that you feel at your peaceful best when you are with them, or you to go to them to suspend yourself from the madness of your routine? It's because you are assured of undistracted and pure love and attention. Think about it.

2. How many times have you said NO to things? How tough is it for you to say no to yourself or to your colleagues or subordinates? We go through life mostly trying to 'accommodate' and trying to avoid confrontation. Saying no is much tougher than saying yes. But remember, the costly lessons in your career came from your inability to say no. I've met people who are stuck in legal problems, some whose careers have gone down the drain, and some who went bankrupt, and the one message I got from all their experiences is, 'I wish I had said no when I needed to.' Why is this relevant to this chapter? Because we go through life being so (seemingly) busy, going with the flow, always in a hurry, always distracted, that we don't think of the consequences of not saying no when we need to.

9

'Stability' Is a Slippery Slope

I'll never forget the day my wife, Zarina, came up with the idea to create UTV's kids' channel, Hungama. At the time, India already had six kids' channels, and children absolutely loved Cartoon Network. Industry experts recommended we should play it safe and not venture into the space. 'UTV's ratings are strong and stable,' they told us. 'Just keep doing what you're doing. There's no need to try something new and risky.' Advertisers echoed the same view and said the market was already overcrowded.

Thank God Zarina didn't listen.

She knew that an authentically Indian brand with smart and original content could win over kids in the age group of four to fourteen. She also knew that the old days of 'slow and steady wins the race' were long gone. She pushed everyone in our team to aim for high professional growth—to stretch and improve individual work skills to tackle a new goal outside our comfort zone. I'm so glad she did. Within two years, Hungama became the number one kids channel in India and was later bought by the Walt Disney Company.

Now, after a win like that, one might be tempted to glide along slow and steady. Instead, she did it all over again and came up with the idea for Bindass, India's first youth channel for those between the ages of sixteen and twenty-four. Bindass went on to be the number one youth TV channel in India and charted a bold, path-breaking approach to youth programming.

The lesson for career professionals is this: ironically, one of the riskiest decisions a professional can make is pursuing a path of 'stable career growth' by trying not to stand out. 'High career growth'—constantly developing new skills and taking on greater work responsibilities—is not only for the super ambitious; it's for everyone who cares about their career.

Is Stable Career Growth Still Possible?

Everyone would love a 'stable' career growth path. It sounds so safe, so secure. No sudden shocks. Slow and steady professional development.

Predictable and guaranteed results for life. What's not to love?

> *'It is safest to go for stable jobs in good companies. After working for nine years, I have saved a lot and it's all for my future. That's the perfect part of working at a very reputed company, you never have to fear that it will crumble. Just focus on building a routine and you're sorted.'*
>
> —Nandita (33), PR professional, Delhi

I believe what Nandita expressed might have been possible in the time of our parents and grandparents. But in the twenty-first century, 'stability' cannot be taken for granted. Put simply, stability is now a slippery slope. Just look at how fast entire industries are rising and falling. If business sectors and companies do not have stability, then how can you trust your job to have it? Think about that. Once you do, you will quickly realize that pursuing high personal growth is the safest way to protect your career and move ahead.

One might ask, 'Do jobs with stable growth even exist any more?' It's a good question. My answer would be that government jobs are probably the closest thing that still resemble predictable and stable career growth. In any country, roughly 10–25 per cent people have, in some form or another, a government job. These public sector jobs are important and beneficial to a country and its people. The main difference is that government jobs have a structured, incremental career ladder to climb. Again, this steady career growth approach is nice for the percentage of people who choose government jobs. But for the 75 per cent of us who work in the private sector, a different approach is needed.

The Riskiest Place to Be Is 5 on a Scale of 1 to 10

If you read my previous book, *Dream with Your Eyes Open*, and someone asks you to rate the book on a scale of 1 to 10, please, please, please do not say '5'. In fact, I would rather you say, 'Ronnie, your book sucked so bad I give it a 2,' than for you to rate it a 5. Why? Because a 2 means at least the book sparked a reaction—even a negative one. But a 5 is just . . . blah. Being in the middle of the scale means you didn't like it and you didn't hate it. In other words, you didn't care either way. A 5 is totally forgettable. It doesn't stand out.

Now apply that idea to your job. A lot of people go to work each day with the goal of being a 5 on a scale of 1 to 10. They try not to stand out positively or negatively. They try not to be noticed in a good or a bad way. In their mind, flying under the radar is a stable and safe career approach. But in reality, nothing could be further from the truth, particularly for mid-career professionals who have been working for ten years or more. Let me explain what Sujal says.

'Personally, I don't see the harm in maintaining a low work profile. I don't always get the highest performance review during appraisal cycles, but my performance isn't in the lowest grade either. It just means I'm not on either extreme with my work performance which makes me feel good.'

—Sujal (26), IT professional, Pune

Here is what I'd like to tell Sujal and all other working professionals. When a boss analyses their workforce, they start by grouping employees into the category of those who stand out and those who don't. For the group that doesn't stand out, the boss then asks, 'If they don't add obvious value, should we replace them with a new hire?' And this is where things get risky for middle-level performers who have not upped their game. Their high salaries mean greater savings to the employer if they fire them and hire a younger replacement for less money. In other words, by trying *not* to stand out and play it stable and safe, they are at greater risk than if they had pursued a high career growth approach through greater responsibilities and lifelong learning to constantly build new skills. Vijay Shekhar Sharma has some key benchmarks for this: 'In the early days of your professional life, you can experiment, but once you're in your fifth or seventh year of work life, you should be concerned if you're hopping jobs for the wrong pulls of salary or title. Look to learn and grow much faster at a steady rate.' And if you're new to the professional world, Harsh Goenka says that's the time to accelerate your learnings. 'It's important to make yourself relevant to an organization when you're young. That's the time to work your butt off. Between the ages of twenty-five and thirty-five is when you make sacrifices and work on learning.' So how can you build high growth traits in your career?

High Growth Trait

We've seen that steady career growth applies to a small slice of available careers, and that taking the middle path of trying to go unnoticed—being a 5 out of 10—is actually *riskier* than striving for high growth at work. So now let's look at what high career growth really means and what it looks like day to day at your job.

Let's start with the basics. When professionals talk about 'high career growth' they are *not* talking about quitting one's job and joining a start-up or becoming an entrepreneur. Instead, the term 'high career growth' means constantly learning and developing new skills while taking on greater responsibilities in the job you already have. Put simply, instead of waiting for opportunities to come your way at work, you create and pursue opportunities. Most of us are hesitant to take on more. But that's where stagnation begins. You may feel overworked in your present task, but picking something new to do and volunteering for it brings a new level of energy and time to make it happen. It's fresh. However full we are after a heavy meal, we always have room for dessert. It's a new taste. Try it. You'll learn, you'll grow and you will be noticed inside your company.

> *'Even if it's a great company, if I don't relate with the product then I won't join purely for the name. For example, RBI (Reserve Bank of India) might be great but it's of no interest to me. I score job openings on three things: quality of work, scope for learning, and the money being offered. Create your own matrix! I think everyone should create their own matrix.'*
>
> —Suhasini (30), brand strategist

I like the way Suhasini thinks. Why, you ask? It's because of her mindset. High growth begins with a person's mindset. High-growth employees view each day as a chance to step up, learn new skills and information, and actively solve problems. They take the initiative at work. They volunteer to pitch in when extra tasks are required. They read industry publications beyond those their bosses ask them to. They watch videos of industry experts and leaders to spark ideas. They take classes to learn the latest methods and software in their field. They are personally invested in jumping over the hurdles in their team's path and figuring out how they can acquire new skills and information to overcome obstacles. In other words, a high-growth mindset forces you to look at your career afresh each and every day.

High career growth is not a one-time event; it doesn't happen in isolation. Developing a high career growth mindset is not about waking up one fine day and saying, 'Enough fooling around. This particular year, I'm finally going to accelerate at work and I'm going to kill it!' No, instead it's about developing a rhythm that lasts many years, and that includes constantly ingesting new information, using that information to develop sharper skills, and applying those skills to solve bigger and more complex problems.

Trust me, once you get into the rhythm of high growth, your job will be safer and more rewarding than just about anything else you could ever do professionally.

One of the reasons some employees resist adopting a high career growth outlook is because they are relatively comfortable where they are now. Some young professionals will say to themselves, 'You know, I'm twenty-seven years old, single, I have no kids, I have a good job and a little extra cash to spend on weekends, and I'm just enjoying my life. There's really no need to put "turbo rockets" on the engine of my career right now.' And for a mid-level professional in their thirties or forties, the thinking goes something like this: 'I've been working several years now. I'm married and we have kids. We can pay our bills each month but there's not a lot left over beyond that. Still, I would rather spend time with the family than on developing extra work skills.'

Both perspectives are perfectly understandable. However, I would strongly advise each of these individuals to flash forward two or three years in their minds. To the younger employee, I would say, 'That's great. But in two or three years do you plan to be married? If so, what about children? And do you think you and your spouse will want to raise children in your current single person's apartment? It's not about where you are right now in your job but where you will need to be in the next few years. Your expenses are going to double, or possibly triple. If you start stepping up at work now, you'll be better positioned to serve your family.'

Likewise, to the mid-career professional, I would say: 'Family life is stable right now, but what about when it's time for the kids to go to college? Or when the bill comes for that wedding?' Mid-career professionals' seniority puts them at greater risk of replacement, because their salary is higher than for a young person right out of college who has been trained using all the latest software and skills. This is no time to be in career-consolidation mode. It's time to fight hard for the family you love so much. The best way to do that is to flash forward in your mind a couple years and ask, 'Where will I need to be then to further my career and honour my personal responsibilities and goals?'

Few things will jolt your desire for high career growth as much as this simple thought exercise.

Attitude Determines Altitude

Someone recently asked me the key attributes I look for when hiring people. It's an interesting question, because you're trying to see the outward signals of a person's inner qualities. There are many important hiring traits, and they vary depending on the position and seniority one is hiring for. But if I were to look at two overall traits of high growth in an individual, they would include:

1) Attitude, attitude, attitude
2) Ability to problem-solve

A high-growth attitude is one where a person listens to colleagues, prepares diligently, and constantly absorbs new information, ideas and skills to bring their very best to each task or challenge in the team's path. Their attitude is optimistic yet realistic. They don't sugarcoat problems or get flustered by challenges. They show respect to everyone, and offer encouragement when the team needs a boost. They know that high growth is a mindset one applies every single day.

Second, high growth professionals are problem-solvers. They understand the company's challenges and face them head on. The DNA of a problem-solver is a person who first *inherits* the team's problems. Their outlook says, '*Everything* is my problem, and I'm going to solve it. I'm not afraid of accepting responsibility, because the team's success *is* my responsibility.' These high-growth individuals don't waste time figuring out who is to blame for a problem, because they're too busy developing solutions. And that's why they get hired and move up. 'I have always hired with an eye on the culture of problem-solving,' says Biocon's Kiran Mazumdar-Shaw. 'It is a cultural thing where I take people who take ownership of their responsibilities, solve problems and move on.' She added that her goal is 'not to be a task-oriented company where people only take instructions', which is why she hires high growth problem-solvers. Attitude and problem-solving—two shining traits of a high career growth professional.

5 Core Takeaways

- Government jobs are the closest thing left that resemble a 'stable' career path.
- That's great, and many do aspire to work in government and public service, which is admirable. For everyone else, a high growth strategy is needed.
- Attempting to remain under the radar at work and go unnoticed isn't a recipe for stability, it's a recipe for danger. Aiming to be average (a '5' on a scale of 1 to 10) is the riskiest place to be.
- Striving for high career growth does not mean one must jump ship and join a start-up or become an entrepreneur. It means developing and sharpening your skills in the job you already have.
- Use the high-growth 'hack' of looking two or three years into the future. Then ask yourself whether your career growth is moving quick enough to meet upcoming personal responsibilities.

When it comes to high career growth, your attitude determines your altitude. How high you fly is up to you. Step up. Take on a little more responsibility. And focus on being a problem-solver—one of the clearest signs you're pursuing high career growth. Do that, and you're in strong shape. And after all, as my mantra goes, if you're a real lifelong learner, you've got very little to worry about.

Call to Action

- I've always walked every step in my life, my work, my personal priorities, my passion and hobbies on my front foot. So decide today, do you walk forward on your front foot, leading, taking control of your destiny, taking responsibility, not wasting time or blaming everyone but yourself; or are you going to work on your back foot—being a follower and having a false sense of stability and security, someone who can get lost as each step is not your own. Remember, walking on your back foot means that in every step of your career you're taking the full body weight. Being on the front foot means more than half the weight is leaning towards momentum, moving forward and towards positivity.
- Do you know why they say 'there are no free lunches'? It's to really say that for everything you want, work for, have an ambition for, there is a price. There is a 'bill' for it.

The ones who do succeed in their work are willing to pay the bill. I've heard so often the false narrative of 'I have the passion', 'I have the burning desire', 'I am really ambitious so I am owed success', 'I work so, so hard that I must succeed' . . . well, sorry to say that all this does not really count—and since it's my task in this book to tell it to you as it is—it's all about whether you are willing to pay the price while having a smile on your face, always. No amount of passion, ambition or jugaad substitutes your readiness to pay the price, and yes, the smile is equally important.

10

From Clashes to Connections

In life and work, conflicts and disagreements are inevitable. The outcomes, however, may sometimes surprise you. Especially when people meet each other halfway and show the other side a little humility and respect.

That was certainly the case when Aamir Khan and I got the news right before the release of *Rang De Basanti* that the heads of the Indian air force, army, navy and defence minister all wanted to review our movie as part of the censor board review process. The reason? The film depicted the death of pilot Ajay Rathod in a Russian MiG crash—and much of the blame for the pilot's death falls on the shoulders of the defence minister.

The censor board and military officials were just doing their jobs; we had great respect for their service. But without their approval, we would be on the hook for a Rs 400 million loss. Equally important, we wouldn't be allowed to release a ground-breaking movie the world needed to see.

Walking into the review meeting that day, it felt like two trains were about to collide. Aamir, the film's director, Rakeysh Omprakash Mehra, and I had all come prepared to respectfully answer and debate tough questions the officials might ask. The movie played for nearly two and a half hours. When the lights came on, Aamir, Rakeysh and I walked to the front of the group and braced for a rigorous interrogation. And then, something amazing happened.

'I thought that was great,' said the army chief. 'I really enjoyed the movie, too,' said the defence minister. 'What's the problem?' The navy chief said he liked the movie as well. Then, the head of the air force spoke. 'Mr Khan, Mr Mehra and Mr Screwvala, thank you for sharing your work with us. I think it's a fine movie. We've never done this before, and we would never censor a movie except under extreme circumstances. You should do whatever you plan on doing. Go ahead and release the film. Best of luck.'

Aamir, Rakeysh and I smiled at each other and breathed a sigh of relief. What could have been a career-crushing conflict had turned out to be a powerful sharing of mutual respect and goodwill. They don't all end that way, of course. But I've learned that sometimes when you go in expecting a clash, you walk out having made a connection.

Good things happen when you try to see things from the other side's point of view and show respect.

See the Other Side

There are so many diverse personality types in a large organization that some of them are bound to clash.

And in smaller companies, people work so closely together it's easy to get on each other's nerves, particularly under pressure. So, if and when you encounter a conflict, take it in your stride.

'I am a part of the middle management and we have it the worst. The pressure of delivering results to my founders has on occasion made me have a nasty outburst at my team.'

—Harman (35), private equity manager, Ghaziabad

If I ever find myself in Harman's situation, I first find a quiet spot and retrace my own words and actions. Did I say a word or phrase that may have triggered that emotional response? Was my tone overly harsh? Was I unclear in my original instructions or expectations? Did I give them the tools they needed to succeed? My goal is to figure out if and where I goofed up. I usually can identify one or more areas where I could have improved my communication or approach. After I identify my role in the conflict or tension, I apologize. That's it.

Look, no one is perfect. We all have the occasional bad day. It happens. 'I'm sorry for xyz' is a powerful phrase, especially when it's sincere. Apologizing shows grace, humility, and that you care about keeping the team strong and united. It also shows people you're not stuck up or proud. Likewise, when others apologize to you, forgive and move on. Extending a little humanity goes a long way.

That's the first step in navigating workplace tensions. See the other side, honestly analyse if you played a role in the conflict, and say you're sorry.

The Words Few Bosses Can Resist

For most of my career I've been on the 'boss' side of the desk. So, naturally, that colours my perspective. But it also means I can let you in on a few secrets about the way bosses think. One of the biggest things that might surprise you is that bosses have the same problems on the way down as you think you have on the way up. In other words, if you think you have peers and team leaders who are tough to deal with, how do you think your boss feels when they have to manage the very same people?

You're not the only one who has to work with them. Your boss does too! So, it starts with knowing that your boss goes through some of the same challenges you do.

> *'Been waiting for a team switch since a year. The two bosses have this ego battle, if you give me X person, I'll give you Y. I am just stuck between this back and forth.'*
>
> —Bhavna (26), marketing professional, Hyderabad

In situations similar to Bhavna's, the key thing to know is that even if you have a bad boss, they still need good people to work for them. As much as you think you need your boss, your boss also needs you. Yes, the competition for jobs is real, and maintaining your edge through lifelong learning and sharpening your soft skills is critical.

But what may surprise you is that you're probably not in as weak of a job security position as you may think. Hiring and training new employees costs a company time and money. There's also the risk that a replacement hire won't be a good fit with the organization's culture—which means starting the job search process all over again. The point is that employers have costs associated with those decisions that put hard-working professionals on firmer ground than one might assume. Bottom line: the caricature of a fire-breathing, dragon-like boss who just can't wait to fire anyone and everyone is silly.

So, assuming you have a relatively 'normal' boss, the questions you want answered are: How do I get my boss to notice me? How can I connect with them? And how do I do all that without sounding like a suck-up? Good questions.

Here's a big secret: most bosses enjoy giving advice and offering wisdom when approached properly. There is a massive difference between asking a person for something and asking a person for *ADVICE* about something. That small and subtle difference can dramatically change the way your boss responds to your requests. The trick is in the way you say it. Here's how to do it. 'Sir, I need your advice on something . . .' Next, state your problem or challenge clearly and briefly. Then, conclude with: '. . . so I've noticed how you help people out and I just wanted to see if you had any advice or guidance on that.' Then be silent. With nine bosses out of ten, you will be amazed at the way that one simple shift of asking for 'advice' opens up a whole new dimension to your relationship.

The 'ask advice' approach also works when you miss a target or deadline. In that situation, you say to your manager or boss, 'I did not meet my target/timelines this month and I've identified what I think were the two biggest challenges.' You then share what the challenges or hurdles were and conclude by saying, 'I wanted to see how you would advise me to solve for those issues so it does not happen again.' This technique works because you confessed that you missed the original goal but, most importantly, you communicated that you realize you didn't perform but have taken the time to think through the reasons instead of blaming the whole world for underachieving. This attitude goes a long way with managers and bosses.

And here's a bonus secret about bosses: if you want to stand out, make your boss look really good. Let them do their work. You do the smart work. Trust me, they'll notice.

Drama Fuels Drama

Perhaps your boss isn't the issue. Instead, office politics, pushy peers and colleagues who love drama are the office hurdles you face.

> *'I heard there was chatter about my daily exit time, and soon after, I noticed I was being given lesser work. Leaving at 5.30 p.m. doesn't mean I was doing bad work.'*
>
> —Shimanti (28), communications manager, Kolkata

Shimanti's experience isn't an uncommon one. In any large company, there are going to be individuals who are known to create problems or launch 'sneak attacks' on people they don't like or feel threatened by. Once you identify your company's drama kings and queens, steer clear of them at all costs.

Choosing 'sides' in office fights is equal to fighting a losing battle. If a colleague is bad-mouthing another employee or wants you to join in gossip, remove yourself from the situation. If that's not possible, say, 'I've never really dealt with her/him, so I don't know,' or, 'They've always been professional with me, so I can't really judge.' By refusing to gossip or bad-mouth others, you protect yourself from being blamed for trashing a fellow employee. It also demonstrates that you value team unity.

The most successful professionals are too busy solving problems and helping the team to get bogged down in petty fights. The more you steer clear of office drama, the more office drama will steer clear of you.

Now, let's be clear: steering clear of drama does not mean you can't or shouldn't be frank and honest when asked for your professional assessment of an idea or strategy. In the early years of your career, you may think it's better to operate under the radar. Maybe you think it's rude or not your place to offer honest feedback. Or worse, you fear it might cost you your job. This is a common mistake many young professionals make. If you're asked for your views or feedback on a project or company initiative, you don't need to be rude or argumentative; you can be honest and offer thoughtful feedback. It will be well received, and you will establish yourself as a straight shooter who is confident enough to offer meaningful insights.

Cronyism, Favouritism and When to Walk

Sometimes drama isn't the issue, cronyism is. In some companies, favouritism, particularly among high-level family members or friends, can be a hurdle in one's career path. And I say this very directly, if you're in a small organization where it's clear that only one or two people are going to get a leadership position, and you absolutely know cronyism will play a role, then it may be time to consider moving on. But if there are thirty people and five of them are going to get promoted but one of them rises due to partiality, don't let that stop you from getting one of the other four posts.

> *'In school, some children were always the ones teachers pick to do everything. Offices are the same; the preference comes out in a more discreet manner but there is preferential treatment.'*
>
> —Jayant (25), technology consultant, Patna

I empathize with Jayant's situation. Partiality and favouritism are frustrating and unfair; the best person for the job should get it, regardless of whether they have insider connections. But I would encourage you to not lose focus and miss out on the other positions of opportunity that *are* available to you. Now, one important difference involves gender unfairness or unequal treatment.

There I think a female professional is much better off seeking help from human resources (HR) and writing to the CEO if she's encountering gender discrimination, because otherwise it's not going to get rooted out and resolved. Today, everyone takes this seriously. Likewise, there must be a zero-tolerance policy against inappropriate workplace behaviour or harassment. Period. End of story.

Be Social, Not Stuck-Up

Confession: I'm more of a homebody than most people realize. I don't drink alcohol, and I've never been a fan of parties. Call me boring, but my idea of a fun Friday night is catching up on a lot of macro reading from around the world that I missed during the week. Or a quiet dinner with family (which for me includes Zarina, Trishya and my son-in-law, Suhail), talking about nothing, and, of course, having fun with my dog Skye. So, if you struggle with the pressure of attending company parties, going out for an after-work drink, or have permission issues due to your age or family commitments, I can definitely relate.

What I've discovered through the years, however, is that there really is value in making an effort to participate in non-work activities. Showing your colleagues that you care about them outside of work is important. It builds bonds of trust and connection, understanding and commitment. Those are important qualities for any team—and they are the people who will keep you sane when the going gets tough. Now, some people say, 'I'm too busy to go out. I have lots of work to do tonight.' And obviously one should never let their performance suffer. But even the busiest person can find a slice of time once every couple of weeks to connect with team members on a social basis. If a person repeatedly says no or that they're too busy, some team members may assume a person is stuck up or think they're too good to spend time with the group. That's obviously not the impression you want to give.

> *'If I am not home right after work ends, my father starts calling every five minutes. I can't explain to him that after work the team goes out for drinks. I don't want to tell my team that at my age I have permission issues.'*
>
> —Sakshi (24), HR professional, Gurgaon

Sakshi's challenge is not her willingness to socialize, it's a practical problem of family restrictions. This is particularly relevant for younger professionals who may still live with their parents, or for those with firm family commitments. Some of these hurdles may be overcome with technology; in the age of COVID-19, social gatherings using Zoom have become quite common. In other cases, perhaps there are reasonable compromises one can make to attend office gatherings that take place at safe times and locations. And lastly, have a chat with your parents—it may take some time, but they will understand as they are concerned about your safety and well-being more than anything else, but they also care about your career progress.

The broader point is that there are no brownie points for being a pariah. It will only add stress to you and your company if you are a phenomenal performer but are not seen as a team player who cares about the people you work with. So, get out of your shell a little bit.

You'll likely find a trusted ear, allies, sources of support and advice or a friend to help keep you steady during times of difficulty.

In closing, I want to say that we all make mistakes every single day. That is fine. The trouble comes when we blame everyone and the company. When one does that, they transform a normal mistake into a failure—more for you than anyone else. When you avoid pettiness and focus on the bigger picture, you win. Every time.

5 Core Takeaways

- Before blaming others for office conflicts, examine whether your words or actions played a role or escalated the situation. Most of the time, 100 per cent of the problem is not on the other side. Taking responsibility for your role in a disagreement will go a long way toward working things out peacefully. And saying sorry does not show you to be weak but in fact builds trust and respect.
- Your challenges may be a lot more like your boss's than you realize. One way to build a connection with your boss is to seek their advice or guidance.
- Avoid getting caught up in gossip, taking sides or office politics. The more you steer clear of drama, the more drama will steer clear of you.
- In the rare case you experience career-stopping favouritism, inappropriate or abusive behaviour, or actions that cross legal or ethical boundaries, report it and change your job if required.
- Socializing with colleagues outside of the office is important. It builds bonds, creates allies and helps you

become part of your company's culture. Try stepping out of your shell. If you have family restrictions, work on reasonable compromises and solutions. Be there for others and they will be there for you.

Call to Action

1. No double talk, no double standards. Whenever I have wanted or expected something from my colleagues, peers, boss, team members or even my wife, daughter or parents, I have first and always set that same standard—with the onus on myself. Lead first, set an example, and you shall receive. Practise this every day and see the respect, response and result you get from others.
2. Ask yourself—are you the one who is more interested in 'getting the job done' or 'getting the credit'?
   Ask this question often. You will achieve a lot more in your career if you figure this out. My best results, the most fun I had at work, was when all of us were so busy doing a great job that no one really cared who got the credit. The victory was so much bigger as it was a team win and the team got the credit. Think about this a lot, and decide how you want this to play out in your career.

11

Batteries and Vampires

Several years ago, during an interview, a journalist asked me for my thoughts on work–life balance. My answer was short and direct, something like: 'If you love what you do, work isn't really a burden.'

Then, as I was writing this book, I spoke with that same journalist again. He reminded me of what I had said, and I admitted to him that my thinking has since evolved. I explained it this way: 'Work–life balance is all about your energy. On the one hand, there are "batteries"—the things that energize you. On the other hand, there are "vampires"— the things that suck energy out of you. Batteries and vampires can be external things such as people or work tasks. Or they can be internal things like feelings of insecurity or fear or moments of clarity or being inspired. You can never totally kill all your vampires. Instead, the goal is to plug into enough "batteries" to overcome the vampires and balance out your energy levels. That's the way to achieve work–life balance.'

Put simply, the most important factor for success is how you receive energy, how you give energy and how you replenish your energy. So, let's learn how.

Identify Your 'Batteries' and 'Vampires'

I don't know about you, but some days I feel exhausted. I've thought a lot about what makes me feel worn out. At first, I thought it might be working long hours. But I quickly realized that that was not it, because sometimes I work a fourteen-hour day and still feel energized and excited, but other times I feel drained after a nine-hour day. The difference, I discovered, is that some days one's vampires overwhelm one's batteries. In other words, some days you have to complete several tasks that drain you without performing the activities that give you energy. For me, vampires have always been interacting with people with a sceptical or negative attitude. I don't get pulled down by problems or situations. Those are challenges to be solved. But if I'm sitting with people whose first reaction is to justify, make excuses, blame everyone and everything but themselves, or with those who are just diffident, always thinking about why something can't be done—that's my vampire time. The worst for me is interacting with those who have a sense of arrogance, attitude of entitlement, or those who only want to give long, rambling lectures or sermons but who have themselves practised very little of what they preach. Thankfully, I spot such people early and avoid them like the plague. Instead, I seek out my batteries, my open-minded, curious, positive attitude, let's-get-it-done colleagues. They inspire me and I inspire them in return. That's great positive energy.

> *'I was at war with my mind, I wanted my mind to work at a certain pace and kept feeling like I wasn't accomplishing as much as my peers were. There was so much still left to do at the end of each day.'*
>
> —Sargam (27), recruitment manager, Bangalore

My advice to Sargam: Start by identifying your batteries and vampires. They can be anything. For example, your batteries might be a colleague or team member who brings out the best in you and gives you a daily overdose of positive energy, or it could be exercise, listening to a podcast or music on your way to work, creating Excel spreadsheets and crunching data, or having fun conversations with peers in the break room. Your vampires are the things that drain your energy levels, such as an argument with a colleague, a stressful project, an ill family member who needs your help, lack of sleep or some relationship drama. Identifying your batteries and vampires is empowering. It forces you to raise your level of self-awareness. Then, the question becomes how best to recharge and boost your energy.

You can define work–life balance in many ways. For example, does balance mean that every single *day* must be perfectly balanced? Every week? Month? I prefer to look at work–life balance on a bi-weekly basis. The reality is that some periods of time are just going to have a lot of vampires. For example, if your team is rushing to hit a tight deadline, you may have several days in a row where you must stay up late and wake up early. Set your own goal to balance your positive energy and the drain you feel when it gets sucked up. Your batteries vs your vampires. You are never going to have ideal days or weeks, but you can set your own cut-offs. If you are having a draining day, or even two draining days, that's manageable, as sometimes you'll have some great consecutive battery days too. But find your balance between your vampire and battery days—maybe it's weekly, maybe it's fortnightly. You have to. It's all about checking in with yourself every few days to see if your energy levels are running low. For me, I have learned to be very brutal with my time, and so my balance has to be mostly in the same day. If the next morning I have not jumped out of bed early—for my morning walk, followed by yoga—I will work on changing my day's plan or meeting schedule to make it largely a battery day.

Remember: it's up to you to make time to boost your energy. Like I said, it isn't something you have to consciously do every day. But you do need to regularly monitor whether your energy bank account is running low. Remember that life has many phases; sometimes work–life balance will be less of a priority, particularly early on, when you are building your career. Vijay Shekhar Sharma put it this way during our discussion: 'All of us have our life in a curve—I believe if before forty you're putting work–life balance as a priority, then you're enjoying a little too much comfort in your life; obviously it depends on your life aspirations. Till a particular point of time, work–life balance doesn't make sense, and after a particular point long days and seven-day weeks cannot be sustained.' That's a helpful way to think long-range about work–life balance as you evolve through the many stages of your career.

One of the biggest drains on our energy may be guilt. A lot of the discomfort one feels related to work–life balance is really about guilt. Guilt for not spending more time with one's spouse, children or parents. You know you can change this anytime you want to. When guilt comes in, balance is out. It does not take too much to get the right balance. It's always the small changes in habits that make the maximum difference.

Many professionals tell me they feel like they can never 'unplug' from their devices because their boss or manager pings them on Slack, WhatsApp, text or email all through the night. This cuts into their ability to rest and have quality family time, which makes them feel guilty. 'Ronnie, I fear that if I don't reply to my boss's 2 a.m. message within fifteen minutes, she will think I'm lazy or fire me. What should I do?'

Firstly, your boss may be demanding, but to expect you to reply immediately at 11 p.m. to a message is disrespectful to you. My sense is this is her way of testing you on 'obedience' versus quality and results. Remember, in the end all that matters is that you deliver on what is really needed to achieve results. So here's what I recommend. For any messages your boss sends you between, say, 9 a.m. and 9 p.m., you should promptly reply with a well-thought-out answer. You want your boss to feel like she has a colleague and team player who actually knows what they are doing—and that even with your boss barking at you, you still think things through and come back with wise and smart answers. Now, as for the 2 a.m. WhatsApp message, keep it unread, because once you read it the expectation is for your boss to receive a reply. Then, at 8 a.m. or 9 a.m. the next morning, reply to the message with a strong and considered response. Let's be clear—if you are diligent and sincere in your work, and you deliver results, your boss will get used to the idea that she has a team member who thinks before hitting reply, takes responsibility, and promptly responds to overnight messages first thing in the morning.

Now, as for your personal life, block some part of the week that is non-negotiable family time. Maybe it is all of Sunday, part of Friday, or at least one evening in the week when you switch off early, by 7 p.m. Whatever works for you is all that matters. Then, really focus on being mentally 'present' in that quality family time. Be active. Make memories. Play. Have fun together. Also, during the rest of the week, if your kids are young, explain to them what you do, why it matters, and why it's interesting and fun. This will help them see that work isn't a negative force but a positive one.

Maybe even take your kids once to your workplace to meet your colleagues and boss. It makes a connection both for your child and those you work with that you are a well-rounded professional for whom family and work go hand in hand and you can balance it all well. One thing I have realized, and especially during the pandemic and work-from-home set-up, is that your parents and spouse expect you to sit down at mealtimes with them. Even if you're hard-pressed at work, this one gesture goes a long way in bringing a smile to their faces. And everyone's got to eat—you can take out some time to sit together and have a breather in the workday.

If you do it right, says Sanjeev Mehta, you can have a fulfilling and multidimensional life. 'When it comes to work–life balance, we must strike a balance between our extrinsic motivations (money, home, fame) and our intrinsic motivator (spiritual, desire to be a CEO, wife/husband and children). You don't want to have a unidimensional life.' It's all about taking proactive work–life balance approaches to help reduce stress, guilt and burnout.

Warning Signs of Burnout

Burnout is bad. It means you've used up your full reservoir of energy, stamina, will to work and positive mindset. You only feel exhausted and have stopped being productive.

Protecting your mental health is critical. By learning how to spot the early warning signs of burnout, you can take control of stress before stress takes control of you.

> *'I've watched my friend have a tough time at work. She would cry on most Sunday evenings because that's how badly she didn't want to go back to work on Monday.'*
>
> —Vipin (31), business development manager, Ahmedabad

Vipin's friend was showing strong signs of burnout. One of the first signs that you're out of balance and headed for a burnout is excessive dread of the week ahead.

Now, I'm not talking about the occasional Monday morning blues; that's normal. I'm talking about feeling physically sick to your stomach Sunday night about the week ahead. Likewise, if you're living for the weekend, that's an early sign that your energy tank is running low. Another signal that you're out of balance is when you constantly feel overwhelmed by your personal life. In the age of COVID-19, this challenge has increased as more and more people find themselves caring for an ill family member or battling COVID-19 themselves. This brings up another point, which is that we sometimes mistake personal stress for work stress. For example, if a person is having family difficulties, it's easy to transfer those feelings of stress to their work life, or vice versa.

Finally, if you're gripped by feelings of insecurity or failing confidence, it could be a sign that you're setting unrealistic expectations or putting unnecessary pressure on yourself. Remember: the things that drain our energy can also be internal. Sometimes the person who causes us the most anxiety and stress is . . . us! Professionals are often harsher on themselves than anyone else. If you tend to 'overthink' things or are a perfectionist by nature, you may discover that you are putting expectations and demands on yourself that your colleagues are not. If you are putting pressure on yourself such that you feel you are pushing yourself way beyond your capacity, you are setting unrealistic expectations. If you set targets or goals for yourself but rarely meet them, even then you are placing undue pressure on yourself with no upside to it.

Remember, the best way to avoid a burnout is to spot the warning signs early so you can rebalance life and work to protect your mind and body.

Don't Hyperventilate, Rejuvenate!

> *'Even when I'm out with a friend, I still keep checking my watch and feel overwhelmed by the volume of work I have left.'*
>
> —Sunaina (27), business development professional, Bangalore

Sunaina, it's time to unplug! Worrying 24/7 won't take you very far.

Take small breaks. Short vacations. Avail of your leave as every time you'll come back with higher energy levels, and your overall year-round performance will increase. I'm a big believer that everyone needs to unwind and get away once in a while. It keeps you fresh. Creative. Rejuvenated. Energized.

Now, you may be thinking to yourself, 'I get thirty days of leave time a year; there is no way I can take all those days. If I did, I might come back from my break and learn I have been replaced. Also, my peers take pride in not using their vacation days. Besides, I actually need some of the money I get from cashing those days out, so I can't afford to use all my leave time.' These are all legitimate concerns. Let's address them one by one.

First, I'm not saying you need to take one long thirty-day vacation. I agree that in today's fast-moving professional world, you may come back and find you've been replaced. So that's an understandable concern. But what about taking three or four days here or there? A mini-break can do wonders to reset your mind and energy.

You can take a few days to enjoy a hobby, says Harsh Goenka. 'People working in consulting organizations work sixteen to seventeen hours a day and are extremely fulfilled and happy. But when I see them reach the age of forty, they are ready to retire! You can face early burnout, or have a lot of issues of mental stress. Therefore, I always think one should have an alternate hobby or outlet. That's extremely important.' For me, in the early days of my work life, theatre and acting were my hobbies and they did wonders. Hobbies or passion projects take you away from work distractions or things you never felt you could take a break from. Later in my career, I made a habit of taking short breaks. Three or four days off to a favourite destination. Writing this book has been a hobby and a great distraction from the daily grind.

Second, I understand that some corporate cultures celebrate people who never take a break. But do you know what your boss values even more? An employee who comes up with the best and brightest solutions. If you take short breaks and come back with greater focus and ideas, no one is going to care that you used your leave days. Results matter most.

Finally, on the issue of cashing out your leave days, I know this is tempting. Mid-level career professionals with a spouse and children often feel guilty if they take their vacation days instead of bringing home extra money for the family. That's a respectable and selfless impulse. However, I would encourage you to think long-term. What's better for your family? Having your mental and physical health at full strength so you can maintain a long and successful career? Or pushing yourself so hard that you crash and burn? Think about it. Consider taking a few short breaks spread throughout the year. They can be an excellent way to refill your energy tank.

Build a Support System

Sometimes we just need to vent and blow off steam. That's normal. And if done the right way it can be quite healthy.

Now, I'm not talking about bitching and whining for no good reason. But someone's sympathetic ear as you talk through the challenges you faced that day or week can be therapeutic.

> *'My wife pointed out one day how exhausted I look all the time. That's when I realized I had been under extended periods of stress and had never accepted or spoken about it.'*
>
> —Swaroop (36), consultant, Mumbai

In Swaroop's case, he found that support in his spouse. Similarly, I would recommend having one or two good buddies at work you can trust. It's best if these individuals are not part of your reporting hierarchy. Everyone should invest in a work relationship where you can support one another, serve as a sounding board to bounce off ideas, and help each other identify signs of a burnout and healthy solutions.

It's all about finding team members, colleagues and even seniors who get the best out of you, inspire you and send you positive energy. Likewise, if you are a team leader or manager, you will have some subordinates who suck up all your energy and make you feel exhausted or like you should end your day right there, versus others who send the positive energy you give them flowing right back to you.

Obviously, you cannot always avoid the people at work who drain your energy, but there are a few 'hacks' you can use. First, talk to those who drain you out about their negative outlook and then give them an overdose of your positive energy. Sometimes, people just need to experience the energizing power that comes through positivity in order to change. Second, if that doesn't work or isn't an option, use an email to lay out your longer thoughts on work matters. This will give you a format to communicate your ideas in an articulate manner without being subjected to constant negativity or energy-draining behaviour.

And while we're on the subject of relationships with peers, I challenge you not to constantly compare yourself to others. There's nothing wrong with being competitive and doing your very best. That's great. But recognize that no two people are the same, and that outward appearances can sometimes be misleading. Focus on being the best version of you that you can be. Your goal each quarter should be to improve on your own personal best. When it comes to your peers, build meaningful relationships with them.

Learning soft skills can sometimes feel like a lonely experience; having friends you can learn from and lean on makes the journey more enjoyable. You will also gain long-term relationships. But don't add unnecessary pressure and stress on yourself by always comparing yourself to others. It's counterproductive and creates unnecessary stress.

Self-Motivation Is Hard Work

Many people view motivation like a magic drug one can take to maintain work–life balance and high energy. Now, let me be clear—I love to hear a motivational speaker or inspiring story just as much as the next person. But, like any drug, the effects don't last forever. Don't get dependent on external doses of motivation. There can never be a steady flow. Instead, the solution is learning the art of self-motivation. This is hard. Very hard. But developing the ability to motivate yourself is powerful and life-changing.

I've spent a lifetime learning self-motivation. I'm still learning. But here's what I've discovered so far. If you're feeling demotivated, you need to ask what's causing it. For most people, demotivation sounds like a reaction to somebody who was critical of you that caused you to feel deflated. But that's not always true. Think of a tyre. Sometimes a tyre gets punctured and deflated by a nail on the road. But other times, a tyre just goes flat because the weather changed, or because of lack of use over time. So, if you're feeling deflated and unmotivated, start by diagnosing the reason.

If it's not something someone said, perhaps it's because you haven't received praise for your work. Everyone needs to hear praise once in a while. But the secret to self-motivation is this: know yourself well enough to be happy with your own internal praise. That takes many years and lots of work and focus to achieve. But it will put you on a path toward achieving a healthy work–life balance.

5 Core Takeaways

- Achieving work–life balance begins with answering two questions honestly: (1) What gives me energy? and (2) What drains my energy? Once you identify your energy 'batteries' and 'vampires', you are on the path to reducing the underlying feelings of guilt that often make work and life feel out of balance.
- Protecting one's mental health means spotting burnout warning signs early.
  These can include trouble sleeping, excessive feelings of insecurity, living for the weekend, Sunday night dread for the week ahead, shortness of breath or physical illness from emotional exhaustion.
- Short breaks are a great way to make 'deposits' in your energy bank account.
  Cashing out your vacation time can be a big mistake. Everyone needs time to refresh.
- Workplace friendships are a wonderful source of support—and an outlet for venting or 'blowing off steam'. Likewise, avoid the comparison trap. Instead, aim to beat your last best performance.
- Motivation isn't a magic energy pill. You have to work hard for self-motivation.
  Figure out what demotivates you, set realistic expectations and then pursue the goals that excite you.

Call to Action

1. Remember, in work and in life things are going to get tough. They are often tough. If you can't handle it,

you're going to be on the sidelines of your career and growth forever. Don't go through life with a sense of entitlement, thinking you need to be dealt a few good cards, or that most times you are not in control of the outcomes and whatever is to happen will happen, so why make things tough and difficult. Well, you're wrong. Because from toughness comes great strength to make things easy. You will always need to make tough choices, be tough on what to give up, face tough work challenges, be tough when things do not work out and be tough to stick it out. Those who think life is easy have a tougher time, and those who accept the reality, succeed with ease and lead a much less stressful life. Think about it.

2. Once, when I came home really early from work, my mom asked me how come I was home at that hour. I was rather vague with my reply. So she asked me wisely (like all mothers do), 'What are you running away from or don't want to face?!' I gave it some thought, but not much. Then, many months later, when I came home really late from work, she asked, 'Who are you trying to impress?' So, what's my point here? It's not about a short or long day. It's about being very honest with yourself, your own work discipline and knowing what is takes to do your best. I've always tried to be very honest with myself on my work deliverables, setting my own standards and goals, and I have found that to be a great balance. This balance allows me to know what I need to get done in a day, week or year. No fuss, no excusing, no blame games—just get it done. I do not need my company, my peers or boss to define work–life balance for me.

12

The One Thing You *Do* Control

I am better than you . . . at failing.

I guarantee it. No matter what you've failed at, I have failed bigger and more publicly than you. In fact, I am so familiar with failure that I wrote a book called *Dream with Your Eyes Open*, where I told stories and learnings from some of my biggest and most spectacular failures. Think I'm joking? The very first sentence of that book starts like this: 'Failure fascinates and intrigues me.' Thankfully, I've also learnt how to push through failure to find solutions. And, as you will see, it's the one soft skill that makes all the difference.

Spoiler alert: you are going to experience failures and embarrassments at many points in your career. It's going to happen. But who cares? So what? Failure is merely the down payment one must give on the way to learning, growth and, ultimately, success. People spend so much time worrying about how they look to others that they forget to ask how they look to themselves. In the end, that's what really matters: whether you believe in your core inner self or not.

Life is unpredictable. But there's one thing in life we *do* control: ourselves. The one constant in life—the one thing we all have direct control over—is our own choices, behaviours and beliefs. Everything else remains uncertain. Economies. Pandemics. Politics. Weather. All those things are in a constant state of change and uncertainty. But your inner self—your self-confidence, self-reliance, self-motivation, self-conviction, self-discipline, self-control, all of it—*that* is the common denominator we all have control over. And since I have more experience with failure than you do, allow me to share some learnings I have collected across many years about how to strengthen one's inner sense of self as you battle setbacks.

The Root of Self-Confidence

Self-confidence is not being arrogant or cocky. In fact, arrogance and cockiness are often signs of a *lack* of confidence. So what is true inner confidence and where does it come from?

Some people are under the incorrect belief that people are either born with self-confidence and self-esteem or they're not. Think about how silly this idea is. What kind of baby emerges from its mother's womb flexing its muscles and strutting around the hospital delivery room with Superman-sized confidence? It's hilariously absurd.

No, the root of self-confidence is knowledge. When you know how to do something, you feel greater confidence in your ability to do it well. From cooking to playing cricket to computer coding—no matter what the task, the more you know, the more confident you feel.

Now let's apply that idea to your career. The problem is that the more years you work in your job, the more you realize how much there is left to learn. Or you may conclude you don't want to push yourself further and are content with your status quo. This can play tricks on your self-confidence, particularly as you hit the midpoint of your career.

'People should also be realistic and not greedy. If you have worked hard for eight to ten years to become comfortable, then now it's time to lay back and be content. Follow your routine and enjoy your life—that's the philosophy I am living with.'

—Rakesh (34), technology manager, Noida

Personally, I don't fully agree with Rakesh's philosophy. By not pushing yourself, you will stunt your own growth which, after some time, will impact your self-confidence. The solution: following a path of lifelong learning to constantly revamp your knowledge. Lifelong learning gives your self-confidence a boost because you're developing and strengthening your knowledge—the very root of true confidence. You have greater belief in yourself because you have greater knowledge inside yourself. And again, it's not built on a false sense of hype, but real learning as you develop new skills year after year throughout your career. Take me, for example. I was very active in creative marketing in my entire media career, yet I felt the need for taking a digital marketing course. I have always valued research and data as powerful tools to constantly sharpen my gut, so I can take better and maybe riskier decisions. A data science course works wonders.

And listen, no matter how good or smart you are, you will experience setbacks. We all do. It's about how you bounce back and grow more confident as you gain new learnings. Vani Kola's advice on this is pitch perfect: 'Life is a continuum of being able to overcome and transcend setbacks. Setbacks have to be looked at as a step-up to your next something. And how you make a comeback from a setback is very, very important. Never feel diminished over a setback.'

Put simply, the shortcut to making your self-confidence skyrocket is to constantly build up your knowledge through lifelong learning and never let setbacks keep you down.

Take Micro Risks First

Lifelong learning builds self-confidence, and that in turn makes us improve our levels of clarity and conviction and our ability to take decisions or risks.

Risk-taking is scary for some people because they fear they might fail. That fear then spirals out of control and grips the mind. *What will my parents think if I try and fail? My friends? My colleagues?* Stop torturing yourself and start teaching yourself.

> *'I get left behind because I take too long to speak up. I have a great idea but I keep picking loopholes in it instead of stepping forward to shine.'*
>
> —Iqra (25), fashion designer, Hyderabad

To Iqra, I would say the best way to learn risk-taking is to start small. You begin with taking a micro risk and build up from there. During work meetings you may remain silent and not share ideas out of fear they aren't good enough. After the meeting is over, you then kick yourself for not having had the confidence to take a chance and speak up. Break the pattern. During the next meeting, take a micro risk by speaking up and sharing an idea. Then, once you see that the world doesn't explode when you take a risk, you will feel more comfortable and self-confident doing it again. Remember, your comment during the meeting doesn't have to be some mind-blowing, world-changing solution. And in fact, if you are a new employee in your first or second year with the company, you may not have had enough time to become a great problem-solver who comes up with big solutions. So relax! Speaking up during a meeting could just mean offering a helpful observation or introducing a useful idea. That's it.

Risk-taking is like building your muscles. You start with light weights (micro risks) and slowly and gradually increase the amount of weight (risk) you're able to lift. Before you know it, you will have strengthened your inner core confidence more than you ever thought possible. Smart leaders know that thriving company cultures encourage risk-taking—even if it results in failure. RPG Group, for example, gives an innovation award for the 'Best Failure'. As Harsh explains, 'We allow failures as long as you learn from them.' Learning through risk-taking and failures—that's the path to success.

Ignore Negative People and Energy

> *'I have a huge fear of "log kya kahenge" [what will people say]. It makes me very uncomfortable and nervous to think that I may come across as foolish.'*
>
> —Milan (27), product developer, Indore

Milan's problem is something I've seen and heard all too often. Let me ask you something. Whose life are you living? Yours? Or someone else's? Life is too short to allow your thoughts and self-esteem to be controlled by negative people and negative energy. Let's address both.

First, negative people. *You* get to decide who gains access to your thoughts, feelings and ideas. If you have 'friends' who constantly tear you down, tell you that you're not good enough or make you feel small—get rid of them. That's not a friend, that's a toxic person who probably suffers from low feelings about themselves. As the saying goes, 'hurt people hurt people'. Look, you're a career professional now. Being an adult means living your own life. Surround yourself with positive people and energy—people who will challenge you to be the best version of yourself possible.

Now, sometimes the challenge to a strong core self isn't other people, but your own negativity. You need to ask yourself—do you have a highly self-critical nature? If the answer is yes, why? Is it because of the factors we discussed earlier, due to false worries about things like where you're from or where you went to school? If so,

I hope we have shattered those myths. But nothing will change unless you do. Let that sink in.

Stop being your own worst enemy. Give yourself permission to believe the best about yourself, not the worst. The self-talk that takes place every day inside your mind is powerful. If you're tearing yourself down with self-critical thoughts or unrealistic perfectionism, cut it out and give yourself a break. While it's great to aim for high-quality work, it is essential not to become so extreme that you don't attempt the task in the first place. Perfectionism is paralysing. It makes you avoid taking risks. It makes you say to yourself, *If I can't do it perfectly then I won't do it at all.*

That way I won't fail or risk embarrassment. Perfectionism also allows people to mask a fear of trying. That's not good.

Remember: the way you talk to yourself inside your mind is powerful. Turn the volume down on negative messages and turn up the volume on positive messages.

Self-Negotiation

Another source of belief in one's self comes through making quality decisions. That means learning to negotiate with yourself. It also means learning to weigh the pros and cons of a decision, deliberate, decide and move forward confidently. Doing this gives confidence in your own judgement. Listen to yourself. Most of the time, your inner voice gives you best advice. The more you listen to it, the more active and sharper you make it. Believe in yourself more than anyone else does.

'I've been working on my pitch deck for my own passion project for a year now. Once it's completely perfect, only then will I seek feedback.'

—Ratna (30), strategy consultant, Dehradun

Ratna, it's time to show some confidence in the hard work you've done and take the risk. The way you sound, you may never make this pitch or get started, and a lot of that is your own insecurity. Self-conviction is always very important and, Ratna, part of getting it perfect is to share it, get feedback and make it better—as getting it right is an iterative process. You need to learn to trust your own instincts and make decisions on your own. This isn't always as simple as it sounds. If you grew up with over-involved parents, or if your parents still try to control your decisions, you may have been conditioned to believe that you can't make decisions on your own. In that case, it's critical that you begin forcing yourself to make decisions independently. Am I saying you should shut down communication with your family? Of course not. What I am saying is that it is your responsibility to push yourself toward self-driven decision-making.

Use the same micro approach we discussed in relation to risk-taking. If it's time to purchase a new healthcare plan or insurance policy, or make a major purchase (such as a car), commit to making the decision for yourself. This doesn't mean you can't get the input and advice of others. What it means is that you will ultimately make the final decision, not someone else. List out the positives and negatives. Gather knowledgeable advice. Then make your decision. Learning to pull the trigger on your own choices builds self-reliance and self-conviction.

And listen, from time to time you will make a decision that turns out to be a mistake. That's okay. You'll learn from it. But most importantly, you will be increasing your own self-reliance.

Never, Never, Never Quit on Yourself

The one sure way to crush your core sense of self is to quit and give up on yourself. When it comes to your belief in yourself, defeat must never be an option. Failures will come and go. But failures are a comma—a brief pause. The key is rolling up your sleeves, pushing yourself, and powering your way through challenges to find solutions.

There is a solution for every challenge one encounters. Now, some solutions are more difficult than others, or may take longer to discover. But there is no problem you or I will face that someone else on planet Earth hasn't already encountered or overcome. That's comforting. It means we're not alone. Our problems aren't special or unique to us—others have faced them, too.

So don't stop believing in yourself. You have the ability to overcome any hurdle. The more you overcome hurdles, the stronger your core sense of self will be. You can't expect others to believe in you if you don't believe in yourself. So do what's necessary to build and strengthen your core sense of self.

Do that, and you will find it impossible to ever quit on yourself.

5 Core Takeaways

- Real self-confidence comes through knowledge—and knowledge comes through lifelong learning. If you're constantly learning, you're constantly refilling your inner supply of self-confidence.
- Build up your belief in yourself by taking risks. It's like strengthening a muscle—you slowly work your way up to lifting heavier and heavier weights (risks), and soon you're stronger than you thought. Start with micro risks and build up from there.
- Silence negative people and energy. Life's too short to allow yourself to be constantly torn down.
- Negotiating with yourself means fine-tuning your own judgement. But that can only happen when you give yourself the permission to try, fail and learn.
- Never, never, never quit on yourself. Ever.

Call to Action

1. What's the opposite of making excuses? It's accountability. We go through most days making excuses, passing the blame on to situations 'beyond your control' (or so you believe), but remember, there is no U-turn on that path. If you continue down it, you're going to be making excuses for the rest of your life—for your work, for your personal life and, most important, for yourself. You change this one single weakness, take responsibility, take accountability, believe that most times you are in control, and you will have changed your life and your career path forever. Make no mistake—it's a very tough U-turn, because

you have spent your whole life fooling yourself that it's not your fault, so changing that thought is really upping your game.

2. From the day I started managing people and then went on to build high-performing teams, I learnt one thing very fast. Find the 'spoilers'—the people in the team, at whatever level, who actually believe that without him/her we would not get things done! The people who have a false sense of self-importance and feel indispensable. Counsel them, but if there is no change in their behaviour, let them go. Ego is good if it gives you confidence, but in most cases ego is a waste of time and teamwork. Walk through life thinking, 'I have all the right answers, I know I am right, I am listening to you for courtesy but actually I've already made up my mind. I did something great last month so I am only slated for greater things!', and you are headed for a train to come hit you. First, ask yourself: Are you even slightly like the person I just described? If yes, your career is going to go sideways in the mid- and long-term. Second, if you have someone like that in your team—or, worse, if it's your boss—then it's time to move on or else she or he is going to make your career graph go sideways too.

13

Seek Guidance, Not Crutches

People often ask me who my most important mentor was. My answer probably comes as a disappointment. I don't have some grand story about a wise guru who took me to a mountaintop and taught me the secrets of life and business. The truth is, I have never had a mentor. I have, however, received mentorship from thoughtful people who asked me hard questions.

Asking meaningful questions is the ultimate mentorship. Instead of telling you what to do, tough questions challenge you to come up with your own answers. They open your eyes to things you didn't see before. And they empower you to take action, not obediently follow instructions like you were forced to in school.

Mentorship is not about taking advice. Had I followed the advice I received over the last thirty years, I would not have made 95 per cent of the personal and professional decisions I eventually did. But whenever I found myself at a crossroads, I was fortunate to have around me people who were willing to ask me challenging questions that forced me to think deeper, sharpen my focus and elevate my game. I'm grateful that they did.

Mentorship is vital and valuable. But it is not without problems. First, let's explore what to avoid. Then we'll discuss the qualities that make a good mentor, how to find the right mentors, seek their guidance and insight, master self-learning, and mentor others when you're ready.

Avoid the Tutor Trap

No matter how old you are, I bet you can still remember the names of some of the tuition teachers you had throughout your school life. I know I can. We all grew up with tutors or test-prep classes. Year after year, these dedicated teachers helped supplement what we were learning (or not learning) in school and college. Math, science, language—whatever the subject, our parents paid for our tuition classes to assist our learning. That was the system we all grew up with.

But we eventually graduate and enter the real world. Suddenly, the assisted learning we depended on from our tuition is gone. Instead, we are forced to shift from assisted learned to self-learning. There's no longer a tutor to prop us up, monitor and review our work, and tell us what to do. Without realizing it, we've fallen into the 'tutor trap' of depending on an older, wiser tutor who constantly holds our hand and guides our path. You've got to break free from these shackles as they were not built to create self-reliance. So now what?

When young professionals land their first job, they typically seek a 'mentor'.

That's not a bad thing; mentorship offers many benefits. But the danger comes when a person turns a mentor into a replacement tutor—someone who becomes a 'crutch' instead of a source of guidance and insight. Read Prathmesh's example and how he views mentorship.

> *'I think an ideal mentor is someone who has the answers to a mentee's tough questions because they have more experience. They can stop us from making mistakes they have made.'*
>
> —Prathmesh (25), MBA graduate, Mysore

Hand-holding isn't helpful. It creates dependency. Before you know it, you're back in the same old tuition mindset, one where you expect to be monitored and have someone double-check your work and correct your mistakes. That's assisted learning, not self-learning. The best mentorship happens when you find someone who encourages you to make your own decisions.

Qualities of a Good Mentor

The qualities and traits of a good mentor may surprise you. First, a mentor does not need to be older than you. Some of the best mentorship I've received has come from younger people asking the most unpredictable and thought-provoking questions. These individuals had a unique perspective that allowed them to ask raw, honest questions—the kind of innocent questions that make you smack your forehead and say, 'Wow! Why didn't I think of that?! That's a game-changer that makes me rethink things entirely.' So, age has nothing to do with being a good mentor.

Second, there's an assumption that a mentor must be a wise expert with tons of experience, someone who has 'been there, done that'. Not true. What really matters is that your mentor thinks differently than you do. This allows them to see things you might miss and consider options you might overlook. For example, if you're highly analytical, a good mentor for you might be someone more intuitive and creative. And vice versa. The point is, a good mentor sees the world through a different lens, which therefore makes *you* see your decisions from a fresh angle.

Third, a good mentor does not need to work in the same company or industry as you do. It's fine if they do, but it's not required. What matters is that you admire their decisions and values. If they take an interest in you, that's even better. But one must not feel limited to only seek mentors from your office or professional specialty. A family member, sports coach, spiritual leader or friend can all potentially make a good mentor if they have the right qualities. And as Vani Kola of Kalaari Capital notes, it's perfectly fine to have 'different mentors for different aspects of your life'.

> *'Initially, I felt my mentor is not guiding me, but after many years I realized my mentor gave me the best guidance because she never made a decision for me. She would simply ask me tough questions for me to reflect upon and ultimately, they would lead me to the right path.'*
>
> —Mahima (36), HR head, Pune

Finally, and most importantly, we all should take away a key learning from Mahima's experience. A great mentor is a strong listener who asks you targeted questions, not someone who tries to control your decisions. Great mentors know that a nudge is better than a shove; helping you find your *own* answers is better than giving you the 'right' answer.

Asking for Mentorship

Okay, so you've avoided the 'tutor trap' mindset, are focused on self-learning instead of assisted learning, and have identified someone with the qualities of a good mentor. What next?

To be clear, you must ask someone to mentor you. It's highly unlikely that someone would approach you and say, 'You know, I've noticed you. I really think you could benefit from talking with me and bouncing ideas and questions off me. So I'd like to volunteer my time and energy to be your mentor.' Good luck with that!

No, the way it works is you must ask someone to give you counsel and guidance.

Don't be nervous about this. Asking someone to be a mentor is one of the biggest compliments a person can receive. So, don't get anxious. Also, don't be disappointed if the person says they're too busy to commit to full-time mentorship. Most people take mentorship seriously and don't consider it a casual commitment.

Here's how to do it.

Approach the person and say, 'Sir/madam, I admire the way you think and the decisions you make. Would you have an hour to grab tea or coffee together? I'd appreciate your insights and mentorship on a few things.' Then, stop and let them speak. Notice that you're not asking for a major time commitment, nor are you asking them to commit to being a long-term mentor. Instead, this low-pressure approach shows that you respect their time, admire the way they think and make decisions, and are not going to become a burden on their already busy schedule. That's the sweet spot.

If they agree to meet with you, come with a focused set of issues or topics you wish to discuss. This lets your mentor know you aren't going to waste their time or ramble on and on. Likewise, stick to the amount of time they agreed to meet. And of course, as with anyone who offers you help in your career, always express sincere gratitude for their willingness to give you their time and counsel. At the end of the first meeting say something like: 'I know how busy you are. I'm very grateful for your time today. I'm going to really think about what you said and the questions you asked me to think about.' They will then likely say you can follow up with any other questions you may have.

Congratulations, you've gained a mentor!

Write Down the Questions Your Mentor Asks You

The time you spend with a mentor is only as valuable as you make it. It's up to you to listen actively and *write down* the questions and ideas your mentor discusses. To help you get the feel and flow of a mentoring session, let's do a rapid-fire example right now. Let's pretend someone named Namrata has come to me for mentorship.

It might go something like this:

Namrata: Ronnie, I need your help. I have this team member who really needs to change her work discipline. I've given her a lot of feedback but it's not working. Should I give her one more chance? Or what?

Ronnie: Let me ask you a few things: how many times have you counselled her? What specifically is she doing wrong?

Namrata: I've only discussed it with her once. But the issue is she's talking over people during meetings. It's becoming a real problem and irritation for the team.

Ronnie: And was that one conversation enough? Were you direct and clear? Or were you tiptoeing around the core issue?

Namrata: I was trying to be diplomatic, so maybe I wasn't as direct as I should have been, now that I think about it.

Ronnie: And now let's assume you had two more talks with her about improving her communication to protect team unity and performance. But she didn't take action and change. Would the company miss her in the job? Or would she be better somewhere else?

Namrata: She definitely adds value and would be missed. I just think she doesn't currently realize how she comes off to the rest of the group.

Ronnie: It sounds like you've identified the core challenge and action items. I look forward to hearing what you do and decide.

Notice that my responses are all questions, never answers. When your mentor asks you questions, write them down. They force you to think through the moves and come up with your own answers and solutions. Great questions from your mentor are pure gold. Treasure them by writing them down.

Pass the Torch

No one ever makes it to the top by themselves with zero help from others.

We all stand on the shoulders of those who came before us. Keep that in mind as you grow and rise, particularly as you enter the middle stage of your career.

> *'In my career of eight years, I've been with the same company and have luckily been mentored by many along the way. As a result, I now mentor many of my colleagues and juniors who have joined the company after me.'*
>
> —Abhijat (30), product manager, Noida

We need more people like Abhijat in the world. Now that you know the qualities of a great mentor and how effective mentorship occurs, be open to passing the torch by mentoring others. Remember, mentorship doesn't have to be a lengthy time commitment; sometimes we mentor others in a short two-minute conversation by asking them a few smart questions.

C.P. Gurnani says everyone should have a 'reverse mentor'—someone younger than you, less experienced, less trained, whom you can help. No one ever forgets their mentors, says Harsh Goenka, and even the best of the best had someone who guided their path to greatness. 'Even when you ask Sachin Tendulkar, he will always credit his coach, his mentor, Ramakant Achrekar. So even the most talented and successful people have had a mentor.'

When you've been on the receiving end of great mentorship, you'll want to do the same for others. Someone asked me why I still try to reply to the hundreds of emails I receive from young professionals. It's because I remember what it was like to be in my twenties and have my questions or messages ignored. We all benefit when we do our best to help pull each other along. You won't always be able to answer every request, and there's not enough time in the day to be a mentor to everyone who asks you. But do your best to at least pass along a nugget or insight to those you encounter. Trust me, they'll never forget it.

5 Core Takeaways

- A mentor is not like the tutor we had throughout school. The goal in a mentor–mentee relationship is self-learning, not assisted learning. Don't grow dependent on your mentor or use them like a crutch. Seek to be mentored, not monitored, so you can chart your own course.
- Great mentors ask thought-provoking questions. Their age doesn't matter. A mentor doesn't have to be

a colleague, have tons of experience, or be an expert. They just need to have an interest in helping you by asking you questions that propel your thinking and decisions forward.

- Asking someone to be your mentor is a great compliment to them.
  Approach a potential mentor with courtesy and respect. Ask for a small slice of their time. Then show appreciation for whatever additional time they offer you moving forward.
- Getting the most out of mentorship requires strong listening skills. Remember, the goal is self-learning. Pay attention to the questions your mentor asks you and write them down. Then think deeply about your mentor's questions to absorb the lessons they contain.
- Once you've experienced the value of mentorship, pass the torch and mentor others. You don't have to make a long-term time commitment. Just ask a few powerful questions to the person you're trying to help. The goal isn't to tell them what to do or give them advice or answers. Just ask questions that nudge them in the right direction so they can discover the answers for themselves.

Call to Action

1. Are you someone who lights fires or puts them out? There are many of us who can so easily go through their whole lives just putting out fires and think they have accomplished a lot, but they have hardly ever lit one. If, after reading this book you have not made enough notes to light more fires than you put out,

reread it all over again ☺. When you light a fire, you give birth to a new idea or a new way of doing something, and that sets off a chain reaction of positive steps with colleagues down the line.

2. Can you count the number of hours and days you've spent till date explaining and justifying why something can't be done? What a waste! Now count the hours you've spent just going out and *doing* it. I am sure it's 100:1. Wow. For every 100 hours you've spent making excuses for why things just can't get done, you spent just an hour on actually *doing* something. Think about it long and hard. Imagine where you would be if that ratio was reversed and was 1:100. Well, it's never, ever too late. Change this ratio and you change a lot for yourself in life.

Afterword

Before you set off on your journey to up your game by sharpening your soft skills through lifelong learning, here are a few words of encouragement.

The goal of this book has been to share my thoughts and experiences that could cut years off your learning curve when it comes to soft skills, and help you stand out and get ahead. You already possess 'hard' skills and knowledge, but today, more than ever, it is the soft skills discussed in this book that make employees zoom to the top.

Part of the reason for this is the lack of such lessons in our education system. And so, like anything that's desired but is in short supply, companies snatch up and reward professionals with coveted talents because they are well-versed in soft skills like oral communication, written communication, storytelling and problem-solving—game-changing traits that an individual can bring to a company.

I believe deeply in the power of soft skills for two reasons. First, I am a product of soft skills and big thinking.

Yes, I went to school and then got an undergraduate degree like everyone else. Education is clearly essential and important. But in the end, from an employer's perspective, that's merely equal to checking boxes on the resumé of life. The real quantum leaps in my career came when I took several years to up my professional game by working on the soft skills mentioned in this book. No one ever taught or told me that these soft skills were the 'turbo boosters' to success. I wish they had! So, with the help of some of the world's best and brightest corporate leaders, I decided to put down all the learnings so you and the next generation will have the running start I never had but wished I did.

The reason it's so crucial to learn soft skills is that they are your best protection against the blinding speed and ferocity of change that industries and global markets will experience in the 2020s and 2030s. The appropriate response to change is never fear, but preparation and focus. If you're constantly upgrading your knowledge and skills through lifelong learning, you're going to be relevant, forward-thinking, and on top of the latest advancements in your sector and specialization. That puts you in a strong career position. Are there any guarantees? No. But while none of us can bulletproof our careers, we can future-proof them.

That's what this entire book is about: giving you insights, wisdom, tips and secrets into the soft skills that will keep you strong, confident and on a constant path of growth, regardless of the oncoming headwinds of global change. Put simply, we feel greater energy, ambition and joy when we know we've upped our game and are capable of winning the race ahead.

When I take stock of my working career, do I think I did anything great or extraordinary to get to where I am now? The answer is 'no'. Outside of the many, many failures that helped me keep my head above water and grow, I would say it was really the huge challenges—the roadblocks and innumerable setbacks that work and life had to offer—that forced me to make incredible sacrifices while giving it my all at levels I did not think existed within me. I stuck it out and persevered where many others would have given up. My sacrifices and the price I paid came knowing that any minute everything I had worked for could be snatched away. I had to keep both feet on the ground, my eyes on the future, my mind at its sharpest, my nose primed to sniff out the winners from the whiners, my ears pricked to be the best listener in the room, while being armed with the power of speech to process all the above and communicate it in the sharpest way for it to be 'contagious'.

For those of you thinking that some people are more privileged and luckier than others, I say with confidence that you can make your own luck by working smart to be in the right place at the right time. It needs patience, self-conviction, a lot of hard work and sacrifice, but it's possible. I was not the typical 'big-city boy'. I came from a lower-middle-class background, but did not waste too much time wondering why some were privileged and I was not. I was mostly focused on ensuring how to make my grass the greenest. There was no room for complacency. It's all about the sacrifices you are willing to make. Sticking it out is ten times more difficult and rewarding than giving up.

While I know my biggest failure is yet to come, I already know that my biggest regret will be if I do not do everything I wanted to do in life—the changes I wanted to make, the stories I wanted to tell, the marathon I wanted to complete, the impact I wanted to create, the one mad thing I always wanted to do but was worried about what others would think, the mindset I wanted to change, the bathroom singer I wanted to be, and, most important, the happiness, balance and family time I always wanted to experience. Start young. Don't spend life regretting anything.

Over the next twelve to eighteen months, commit to work on one or two of the soft skills in this book. Take time to go deep with each skill. Then repeat the cycle. Remember, lifelong learning is a marathon, not a sprint. So, don't feel the pressure to learn everything all at once. It's taken me and the thought leaders featured in this book our entire careers to learn these skills. In fact, we're *still* learning them! So, go slow, have fun and enjoy the journey.

Finally, you'll want to reread certain chapters in the book from time to time. At different stages of your career, the impact of these learnings will mean different things to you. As Heraclitus said, 'No man [or woman] ever steps in the same river twice, for it's not the same river and he's not the same man.' The meaning of this book will evolve as you do.

My challenge and hope for you is that you realize you are capable of more than you ever thought possible. The only real limits are those we impose upon ourselves. Everything else is just noise. Never allow someone else to control or diminish your goals and ambitions. Surround yourself with positive people. There is no better winning formulae than a positive one—give it all you've got.

Attitude is everything. The first person to do something out of the ordinary is always viewed as 'strange and weird'. Many may even laugh at him. But soon one more joins him, and more follow; this swells into a crowd or even a herd, and slowly but surely, the one who started it all goes from being weird to a visionary. Try and be that person.

Your time is now, so rise. Commit. Listen. Sacrifice. Prepare and plan. Want it badly. Empathize. Learn to say no. Communicate and, most importantly, bring fun, joy and pride to everything you do.

Enjoy the lifelong learning adventure.

Up your game! And go KILL IT.